Contemporary
Christian Issues

by

Christian Scott Anderson

Contemporary Christian Issues

Christian S. Anderson

Apologetics Boot Camp

Outline of Contents

I. Spiritual Gifts: Did God Give Them An Expiration Date?

    Introduction

    Old Testament Precursors To Spiritual Gifts

    The Work of the Spirit In the Intertestamental Period

    Spiritual Gifts In The New Testament

    The Permanence of Spiritual Gifts

    Speaking in Other Tongues

    Conclusion

II. Israel And The Church: Did God Say *Lehitra'ot* To Israel?

    Introduction

    God's Promises to Abraham

    The Land Lost, Regained, Lost, and Regained

    The Jews are a Sign of God's Faithfulness

    Conclusion

III. The New Atheists: How Do We Answer Them According To The Bible and Logic?

Introduction

Answering Atheists New and Old

Atheism Represents An Inadequate Worldview

The Bible Agrees with Reason

Conclusion

IV. Conspiracies: What Should Be The Christian Response?

Introduction

The Moon Landing Conspiracy

The Flat Earth Conspiracy

Miscellaneous Conspiracy Theories

The Chemtrail Conspiracy

The JFK Assassination Conspiracy

The Protocols of The Elders of Zion Conspiracy

Conclusion

V. Aliens And UFOs: Are ETs and Little Green Men (LGM) Biblical or Logical?

Introduction

Isn't it possible that God could have created other worlds with intelligent   life?

The Bible mentions the translation of Enoch (Gen. 5:24), and that Elijah was carried off by a "chariot of fire" (II Ki. 2:11). Couldn't these references be referring to alien abductions couched in terms the ancient Bible writers would understand?

Isn't it possible that Ezekiel's vision (ch. 1, vss. 4-28) was actually his sighting of an alien spacecraft?

Conclusion

VI Sex and Gender: What Does The Bible Say?

Introduction

Gender and the Bible

Biblical Sexuality

Conclusion

Glossary of Terms

References

I. Spiritual Gifts: Did God Give Them An Expiration Date?

Introduction

It may seem odd that a phenomenon that manifested itself two thousand years ago could be a contemporary Christian issue. However, ever since modern outpourings of the Spirit were witnessed in the early 20th century in widely diverse regions of the earth (South Africa, Norway, Wales, and Los Angeles, California, etc.), established churches have spoken against these moves of the Spirit and have even sanctioned members who have claimed the experience for themselves.

Common arguments against the permanency of spiritual gifts are based on the idea that they were bestowed only as foundational aids for establishing of the church. When the New Testament was finally compiled and orthodox doctrine universally recognized, the direct influence of God over His church by means of the *charismata* was no longer deemed necessary.

Vine (pg. 1155), though speaking mainly about the gift of tongues, actually represents entirely the views of the cessationists in this statement:

"There is no evidence of the continuance of the gift after Apostolic times nor indeed in the later times of the Apostles themselves; this provides confirmation of the fulfilment [sic] in this way of I Cor. 13:8, that this gift would cease in the churches, just as would "prophecies" and "knowledge" in the sense of knowledge received by immediate supernatural power (cp. 14:6). The completion of the Holy Scriptures has provided the churches with all that is necessary for individual and collective guidance, instruction, and edification."

A similar idea is held by B. B. Warfield. He surmised that supernatural gifts of the Spirit were bestowed in order to authenticate the apostolic office. A sign of an apostle was both possession of these gifts and the power to confer them on those who have confessed Jesus of Nazareth as Lord and Savior (*Miracles: Yesterday and Today*, pgs. 6-21).

According to Warfield, the gifts operated in the church until the passing of the apostles. They ceased altogether with the death of those upon whom the apostles had bestowed them, in other words, within a generation or two following the Day of Pentecost (ibid., pgs. 3, 21ff).

W. H. Griffin Thomas viewed the spiritual gifts as a divine testimony to the nation of Israel of Jesus' messianic office. The gifts were no longer apropos following Israel's rejection of the Gospel (*The Holy Spirit of God*, pgs. 48ff).

It has been argued that these views are reconciled by distinguishing between those miraculous manifestations meant to be signs (Grk. *semeia*) accompanying a new revelation, that were given specifically to the apostles for the evangelization of the Jews and Samaritans (see Mk. 16:17ff; Acts 2:19 & 43; 4:16, 22 & 30; 5:12; 6:8; 8:6 &13; 14:3; Rom. 15:19; II Cor. 12:12; Heb. 2:3ff), and those spiritual gifts meant to edify the largely Gentile church (see I Corinthians, chaps. 12-14).

Those who advocate the permanency of the spiritual gifts in the life of the church ascribe their decline and eventual near disappearance to a lack of faith, that pastors and teachers were relying on their own abilities instead of God's power. This group sees the rise of the church as a hierarchical *organization* rather than an *organism* as the true reason for the near extinction of spiritual gifts. The original church, as viewed by the Apostle Paul, is a body, a living thing composed of members possessing spiritual gifts he likens to the anatomical parts of a physical body (I Cor. 12:11-28). Moreover, this camp claims the gifts have been rediscovered at various times, especially during periods of spiritual renewal.

The cessationists, as those who deny the permanence of spiritual gifts are called, rely on a single verse to back their claims:

> "Charity never faileth: but whether *there be* prophecies, they shall fail; whether *there be* tongues, they shall cease; whether *there be* knowledge, it shall vanish away (I Cor. 13:8)."

However, as long as God has been dealing with mankind through a covenant people, He has used the miraculous to authenticate His word, heal, provide, exhort, predict the future, and bring comfort.

.

Old Testament Precursors To Spiritual Gifts

Of course, the greatest of all miracles is the creation event itself (Gen. 1:1ff), but that is outside the scope of this study. There are other Old Testament miracles that do not quite correspond to the spiritual gifts of the New. For example, we can't find a New Testament miracle quite like Aaron's rod turning into a serpent (Ex. 7:10-12), though the Apostle Paul did shake a venomous one off into a fire that had fastened onto his arm, suffering no ill effects in the process (Acts 28:5 & 6).

Signs, wonders, and spiritual gifts in the New Testament have corresponding ones found in the Old. There are healings (Gen. 20:17), works of wonder (II Ki. 6:5-7), prophecy (I Ki. 22:15), wisdom (Ex. 31:1-6), and the word of knowledge (II Ki. 5:26 & 27). Even the gift of tongues is hinted at in the eerie handwriting on the wall of a Babylonian king's palace (Dan.5:5-29).

The MENE MENE TEKEL UPHARSIN of the passage, while not strictly a message in tongues, is very much like it. Literally it reads, "a mina, a mina, a shekel, divided," but Daniel's interpretation rightly predicted the overthrow of the Babylonian Empire by the Persians. Daniel informed Babylonian king Belshazzar, "You have been weighed in the balances and found wanting... Your kingdom is divided, and given to the Medes and Persians" (vss. 27 & 28).

According to the Apostle Paul, even the gift of tongues itself was foretold in the Old Testament: "With *men* of other tongues and other lips will I speak unto this people; and yet for all that will they not hear me, saith the Lord" (I Cor. 14:21). Paul quotes Isaiah 28:11. Although his use of the quote seems strained, we have to remember the mere *words* of scripture always had the force of an argument with Jews, regardless of their literal meaning or context.

The Holy Spirit (Heb. *ruach qodesh*) came upon various individuals in Old Testament times to confer upon them a skill to accomplish tasks like craftsmanship (Ex. 31:3) or leadership (Judg. 3:10), or for supernatural physical empowerment (Judg. 14:6).

The Holy Spirit operated in the prophets of Israel to predict, proclaim, inspire scripture, and foretell the coming of the Messiah. The kings of Israel were filled with the Spirit to overcome the enemies of Israel. For example, the Holy Spirit came upon King Saul when Nahash the Ammonite threatened the people of Jabesh-gilead (I Sam. 11:3). Saul even prophesied when the Spirit of God came upon him on two separate occasions (I Sam. 10:12; 19:24), such that it became an byword: "Is Saul also among the prophets."

The Work of the Spirit In the Intertestamental Period

The 400 years between the testaments are often called "The Silent Years," since no prophetic voice arose from Malachi (about 400 BC), "the last prophetic voice of the OT" (Unger, pg. 450) to the advent of Jesus. During this era, the production of Holy Writ had been suspended. As a consequence, this period saw a paucity of miraculous workings of the Holy Spirit, since miraculous events accompany revelation as signs confirming it.

A notable exception to this occurred during the rededication of the Temple after the Maccabees, under Judas son of Mattathias, drove out the forces of Antiochus Epiphanes in 164 BC. Only one undefiled cruse of oil was available, enough for one day, but this one day's supply of oil was miraculously lengthened to accommodate the full eight days necessary for the cleansing of the Temple. The miraculous multiplication of the oil is celebrated on the eight days of the Jewish holiday celebrated in December. This festival is known as the Feast of Lights or *Chanukah*.

God's people during this period looked backward nostalgically to the time when God moved supernaturally in miraculous deeds through His prophets and servants. However, it was also known that God had promised that at some point yet future He would pour out the *ruach qodesh* again upon His people (Ezek. 36:26; Joel 2:28 & 29). They clung also to this hope:

> "And there shall come forth a rod out of
> the stem of Jesse, and a Branch shall grow
> out of his roots: And the spirit of the
> LORD shall rest upon him, the spirit of
> wisdom and understanding, the spirit of
> counsel and might, the spirit of knowledge
> and of the fear of the LORD" (Isa. 11:1 &
> 2).

There seemed to have been no present rejoicing in the work of God's Holy Spirit. However, there was some indication of the moving of the Spirit among the Essenes and other sects prior to the advent of the Lord Jesus.

Spiritual Gifts In The New Testament

The English term "spiritual gifts" is the common rendering of the Greek plural noun *charismata*. It is related to the word *charis* ("gift, grace"). Hence, the term may more accurately be translated "grace-gifts." The singular form of the word is found in Rom. 1:11; 5:15 & 16; 6:23; I Cor. 1:7; 7:7; II Cor. 1:11; I Tim. 4:14; II Tim. 1:6; I Pet. 4:10. The plural form is found in Rom. 11:29; 12:6; I Cor. 12:4, 9, 28, 30 & 31.

The plural form is used principally in the sense of the supernatural gifts bestowed on Christians for service. This was foretold by the prophet Joel (2:28) and confirmed by Christ's promises to His disciples (Mk. 16:17; Jn. 14:12; Acts 1:8).

Spiritual gifts are distributed by the Holy Spirit according to His sovereign will (I Cor. 12:11). A believer may receive one or more gifts (I Cor. 12:8ff; 14:5, 13).

.A list of the spiritual gifts is found in I Corinthians chapter 12, verses 8-10:

> "For to one is given by the Spirit the word of wisdom; to another the word of knowledge by the same Spirit; To another faith by the same Spirit; to another the gifts of healing by the same Spirit; to another the working of miracles; to another prophecy; to another discerning of spirits; to another *divers* kinds of tongues; to another the interpretation of tongues."

This list is not complete, Paul mentions additionally ministry, teaching, exhortation, ruling, and mercy (Rom.12:6-8). However, the aforementioned five gifts are not really those disputed by the cessationists. Even the most ardent anti-Pentecostal, hard-shell Baptist would not begrudge the Christian church the likes of teachers or exhorters, and none would dispute those who possess the quality of mercy.

Cessationists, by in large, are not averse to words of wisdom or knowledge, and none of them would dispute the reality of faith. Cessationist churches have even been known to offer prayers for the sick! Do they do so without the expectation of healing? So, when we get down to cases, we find the cessationists really have a problem only with the gifts of I Corinthians chapter 12, verse 10, to wit: working of miracles, prophecy, discerning of spirits, tongues, and the interpretation of tongues.

Cessationists cannot really dispute the reality of the miraculous. If they belong to churches that preach the Gospel, that is, the deity, atoning death, and resurrection of Jesus of Nazareth, the supernatural changing of lives ought to be evident. Every life changed by the Gospel is a miracle. Cessationist churches sometimes have missionaries speak from some of the most backward areas of the world. They declare categorically the fact of miracles on the mission field. So, miracles cannot be denied, even by anti-Pentecostal, hard-shell Baptists.

What about prophecy? Prophecy itself is not primarily a foretelling of future events. The lexical meaning of *propheteia* in Classical Greek is "the gift of interpreting the will of the gods," and secondarily, "the gift of expounding scripture, public instruction, preaching." The verb form, *prophetuo* is defined in this manner: "to expound publicly, preach." A prophet (*prophetes*) is "one who speaks for another: an interpreter of the will of the gods." Poets were called *Mouson prophetai*, or "interpreters of the Muses." So, a prophet is generally, "an interpreter, proclaimer," secondarily, "an interpreter of inspired scripture, preacher." Only lastly is a prophet defined as a "foreteller" or predictor of future events (Liddell & Scott, pgs. 611 & 612).

In the New Testament prophecy, according to Vine (pg. 893) "signifies a speaking forth of the mind and counsel of God." He says further:

> "Though much of O.T. prophecy was purely predictive, see Micah 5:2 e.g. and cp. John 11:51, prophecy is not necessarily, nor even primarily, foretelling. It is the declaration of that which cannot be known by natural means, Matt. 26:68, it is the forth-telling of the will of God, whether with reference to the past, present, or future, see Gen. 20:7, Deut. 18:18; Rev. 10:11; 11:3...."

Do cessationist churches object to those "rightly dividing the word of truth" (II Tim. 2:15), that is, interpreting scripture? Obviously not. So, we can add another spiritual gift, that of prophecy, to the permanent column that cessationists insist has been done away.

Three gifts to go.

Now the discerning of spirits would be considered "weird" even by many confessing Christians, but the reality of a dark realm of "principalities and powers" (Rom. 8:38; Eph. 3:10; 6:12; Col. 2:15) populated by evil spirits is so evident from the teaching of scripture, that it cannot be denied (Lev. 17:7; Deut. 32:17; II Chron. 11:15; Ps. 106:17; Mt. 8:29; Mk. 1:24; 3:11; 5:7; Lk. 4:34, 41; Acts 19:15; I Cor. 10:20; Jas. 2 :19; Rev. 9:20).

Would any cessationist who has studied the Bible and believes its words doubt the existence of evil spirits and their wicked sovereign? We would have to conclude, no. Furthermore, would a Bible-believing Christian of any sort doubt the means of detecting the presence of these evil beings? Again, that would be another negative.

So, we are left with the final two spiritual gifts/graces. It is obvious the speaking in other tongues and the interpretation thereof are really what our cessationist friends bristle about.

So, cessationists *don't actually believe in the cessation of all the spiritual gifts.* When we get right down to it, they only truly object to the last two. However, since the interpretation of tongues is really dependent on the gift of tongues, that gift is really the only one that the cessationists would declare "ceased."

The Permanence of Spiritual Gifts

It is obvious that spiritual gifts have never really ceased in the life of the church. Healing, miracles, faith, and the like have never faded away, at least not entirely. There is nothing in scripture to indicate cessation of the spiritual gifts. The Lord Jesus told us that miraculous signs would follow those who believe (Mk. 16:17 & 18). No end date for these signs is indicated, "*these signs **shall** follow them that believe.*"

The Reformation initiated by Martin Luther in 1517 was really a move of God. It was a revival of the church after centuries of dead ritual and empty tradition. This man insisted on the preaching of the word of God and its proper exposition. That has always been the key to revival, along with an insistence upon spreading that word through evangelization and missions. During the Reformation there were reports of miraculous deeds, prophecy, and the speaking in tongues, though these manifestation were often abused and were thus consequently condemned.

The abuse of spiritual gifts seems to be a principal argument against them in the modern church by cessationists. Even the Apostle Paul gave instruction against the abuse of the gift of tongues (I Cor. 14:23).

However, he does not "throw out the baby with the bath water."

The Great Awakening (1734-1744) is the first recorded revival in U.S. history. It was a genuine move of God during which gifts of the Spirit were manifest, though we have little evidence of speaking in tongues (Grk. *glossalalia*). It was followed by a period of unbelief, fueled by English Deism and the spirit of infidelity stirred up by the French Revolution. A Second Awakening beginning in 1797 checked this trend. The Great Revival began in the early 1800s and continued until about 1830. During the 1850s there was another revival based on prayer meetings conducted by laymen in America's urban centers. The Holiness Revival began in the late 1800s. The Holiness Revival may well be the direct precursor to the outpouring of the Holy Spirit experienced by attendees of the Azusa Street Revivals in downtown Los Angeles.

From the days of Jonathon Edwards and George Whitefield cold Christian hearts have been rekindled and converts have been made by gifted preachers of the Gospel exercising the gift of prophecy, i.e., interpreting the word and speaking on behalf of God and His Son. Nearly every generation has had these representatives of Christ stress the need to be twice-born by means of receiving the Holy Spirit.

Asahel Nettleton was a successful Congregational evangelist, beginning his ministry in 1812. Twelve years later Charles Finney (1792-1875) began his preaching career. He continued in this work until 1860. Finney was the first to utilize the "altar call," i.e., an appeal to anyone who wished to be saved to come forward in the meeting hall and make a public declaration of faith in Christ.

Finney's altar call and the mourners' bench of the Holiness Movement would be indispensable tools in the "tarry sessions" that would see many receive the baptism in the Holy Spirit evidenced by the speaking in other tongues some years later.

Dwight L. Moody (1837-1899) and Ira Sankey (1840-1908) started joint revival work in 1871 that lasted more than 20 years. They visited most of the large cities of the United States and Great Britain and preached literally to millions before the advent of radio and television.

Billy Sunday (1863-1935), was a professional baseball player who began his career as an evangelist in 1896 and preached into the 20th century. He was followed by the ministry of Aimee McPherson (1890-1944). She founded Angelus Temple in 1923, Life Bible College (1925), and the Church of the Foursquare Gospel in 1927. McPherson definitely practiced the laying on of hands for healing and anointing with olive oil (Jas. 5:14), and a great many testified to having received a supernatural healing of various ailments. Her services also saw the outpouring of the Spirit followed by the evidence of speaking in tongues.

But McPherson's efforts had an antecedent. In 1906 a remarkable event occurred in downtown Los Angeles in the state of California During a series of revival meetings on Azusa Street, an outpouring of the Holy Spirit was followed by many receiving the gift of speaking in tongues, as was witnessed during the Day of Pentecost in Acts, chapter 2. There were similar outpourings during this time in such far-flung places as Norway, South Africa, and Wales.

This Pentecostal Revival brought about many innovations that have been adopted by non-Pentecostals. "Churchy"--sounding music was replaced by that having more of a contemporary beat. Pipe organs were replaced by guitars and drums, and the worship was freer and more spontaneous. The Jesus Revival of the late 1960s to early 1970s saw the introduction of music with a rock-and-roll beat, but many of the dropouts from society at the time known as Hippies were drawn by that to faith in Christ by such gifted preachers as the late Chuck Smith.

However, these efforts were lubricated by the "oil" of the Holy Spirit. It is highly doubtful that these works of McPherson, Smith, and other preachers would have born the fruit they did without the emphasis of the baptism of the Holy Spirit and the bestowal of supernatural gifts, especially that of speaking in tongues.

So, it is evident that the Reformation and the revivalism that it later spawned opened a door for future outpourings of the Holy Spirit. It is no accident that Pentecostal churches have been the main driver in the 20th and 21st centuries for mission work that has brought the Gospel to the most remote parts of the world. These efforts are a direct consequence of those receiving the baptism of the Holy Spirit.

Speaking in Other Tongues

Since speaking in tongues is such a prominent part of this discussion, it is prudent that we give it a detailed discussion.

Speaking in tongues was promised by Jesus before His ascension (Mk.16:17). On another occasion the Risen Lord said, "Not to depart from Jerusalem, but wait for the promise of the Father" (Acts 1:8); "For John truly baptized with water; but ye shall be baptized with the Holy Ghost not many days hence" (vs. 5).

The time of this outpouring occurred on the Day of Pentecost. This day celebrated the completion of the barley harvest, which began when the sickle was first put to the grain (Deut. 16:9). Its observance was indicated in the time of Solomon (II Chron. 7:13) as the second of three harvest festivals (Deut. 16:16). This second harvest festival occurred about fifty days after Passover.

During the Intertestamental Period and later, Pentecost was celebrated as the anniversary of the giving of the Law (Jubilees 1:1). The Sadducees insisted on celebrating it on the fiftieth day from the first Sunday after Passover (assuming the Sabbath of Lev. 23:15 to be the weekly Sabbath). Hence, this reckoning was made the law of the land while the Temple stood, However, the Pharisees interpreted the Sabbath of Lev 23:15 as the Feast of Unleavened Bread (Lev. 23:7). So, the Pharisaic reckoning became the rule in Judaism after the destruction of the Temple in 70 AD.

Pentecost is associated with *harvest*. Harvests are also an indication of abundance and blessing. Furthermore, harvests in ancient Israel were occasions of great rejoicing. In fact, God *commanded* the Israelites to rejoice (Deut. 16:14):

"And thou *shalt* rejoice in thy feast, thou
and thy son, and thy daughter, and thy
maidservant, and the Levite, the stranger,
and the fatherless, and the widow, that
are within thy gates" (emphasis added).

The *shalt* in the text is a jussive future. In other words, it
is equivalent to an imperative, a command (see Ex. 20:3-
17).

So, when the disciples of Jesus were baptized in the Holy
Spirit on the Day of Pentecost, their display of speaking
in tongues was mistaken for being "full of new wine"
(Acts 2:13). That they were thought to be tipsy is an
indication the disciples were "drunk on the Holy Spirit"--a
condition of being so filled with the Holy Spirit that the
one filled actually feels inebriated and appears to be so
by observers. However, the Spirit-filled "inebriant" is
actually fully in control of his or her self. Being filled with
great joy is also part of this infilling.

And with this outpouring of the Holy Spirit there was a
great harvest. Peter preached the atoning death,
Lordship, and resurrection of the Jesus of Nazareth. A
formerly timid Peter spoke boldly after receiving the
baptism in the Spirit with evidence of speaking in
tongues. The onlookers were cut to the heart (Acts

2:37), and exclaimed, "What shall we do?" Peter admonished them to "repent, and be baptized every one of you in the name of Jesus Christ for the remission of sins" (vs. 38). Those who received the words of Peter's discourse were baptized that very day, and they numbered about three thousand souls (vs. 41).

The baptism in the Spirit was prophesied in Joel chapter 2, as we have mentioned. However, that the out-pouring of the *ruach qodesh* was not just to be an end-time blessing for Israel alone. The LORD declared, "I will pour out my spirit upon *all* flesh" (vs. 28).

In the beginning the Spirit fell upon Jews only until Philip, one of the seven deacons of the church at Jerusalem (Acts 6:5) began preaching to the Samaritans, a people mixed as a result of the policy of Assyrian king Sargon, who conquered the northern kingdom of Israel, deported some 27,000 Israelites, and moved in colonists from various parts of his empire (II Ki. 17:24). Philip's preaching brought great results, there were conversions, exorcisms, and healings in the city of Samaria: "And there was great joy in that city" (Acts 8:8). The Samaritans believed, but they had not received the Holy Spirit until Peter and John traveled there and laid hands on them. They then received the Holy Spirit (vs. 17). It does not mention speaking in tongues, though we can assume that manifestation, else how would we distinguish the subsequent spiritual phenomenon from the former?.

However, a most momentous event occurred sometime later when Simon Peter received a vision while lodging in Joppa. In the vision were all kinds of unclean beasts, and he was instructed, "Rise Peter, kill and eat" (Acts 10:13). As a completely observant Jew, Peter refused, but the Voice in the vision declared. "What God hath cleansed, *that* call not thou common" (vs. 15). This was the divine opening of the Gospel to the *goyim*, the Gentile nations, for at the same time Peter was receiving his thrice-seen vision, a delegation supernaturally sent from the house of the centurion Cornelius arrived from Caesarea (vs. 17).

Cornelius was a God-fearer, that is, a Gentile who had a hunger for the true God, but for one reason or other, most likely social ostracism, would not submit to the rite of circumcision. Gentiles could attend synagogue, though they were required to stand in the back near the entrance. Gentiles could visit the Temple, but they were also restricted there to the Court of the Gentiles.

So, a barrier existed between the God of Israel and the Gentiles. However, their conversion had been predicted centuries before: Isa. 11:10; 42:1; 49:6; 62:2; Jer. 16:19-21; Hos. 2:23; Mal. 1:11; Mt. 8:11 & 12. Jesus declared that "other sheep I have, which are not of this fold: them also I must bring" (Jn. 10:16), and to certain Greeks who had come to the Temple to worship, He said to them, "If I be lifted up from the earth, will draw all men unto me" (12:32). The crucifixion of Christ ushered in a new era that would see Gentile and Jew worshipping one Lord.

However, this barrier was removed at the house of Cornelius as he preached Christ's atoning death on the cross and resurrection from the tomb (Acts 10:34-48). While Peter was preaching his message, the Holy Spirit fell upon uncircumcised Gentiles, and they did "speak with tongues and magnify God" (vs. 46).

So, in the beginning tongues functioned as a *sign* that God had accepted Gentiles as members of the covenant community. However, the *glossalalia* at Corinth differed from that witnessed at Jerusalem, Caesarea, or Ephesus (Acts 2, 10, & 19). The Acts occurrences saw entire companies break into tongues after being baptized in the Holy Spirit. At Corinth the gift of tongues was not given to everyone (I Cor. 12:10, 30). Tongues as a sign seemed to be foreign languages supernaturally understood by the hearers. Again, at Corinth the gift of tongues required an additional gift of interpretation in order to be made intelligible (vss. 5, 13, & 27). In any case, *glossalalia* are everywhere seen as utterances inspired by the Holy Spirit and used to glorify God (Acts 2:11; 10:46; I Cor. 14:2, 14-17 & 28).

It might be said that speaking in tongues represents kind of a "prayer 2.0." When interpreted properly, they have a prophetic element. The interpreter can exhort, encourage, or rebuke. Praying in tongues strengthens the prayer and opens the doors of heaven to his or her soul. Those possessing this gift sense that praying in tongues covers all the bases of that which needs prayer. Praying in tongues, as does all prayer, calms a turbulent spirit, but seems to do so *immediately*. It paves the way to evangelism, and builds bridges from one culture to another. The history of speaking in tongue in the church has always been followed by expansion and growth. So, why anyone would object to such a gift is a mystery.

Conclusion

A principal cessationist argument against the charismatic gifts is their abuse. They look at the likes of the grifting "blab-it-and-grab-it" prosperity pulpiteers as proof that spiritual gifts are fake, or have an even more sinister origin--that they are downright satanic! However, what move of God has not been abused by overly enthusiastic, but sincere Christians, or by charlatans who attach themselves like leeches to the body of Christ?

In Paul's day he observed that some were preaching Christ out "of contention, not sincerely" (Phil. 1:16), but "whether in pretense, or in truth, Christ is preached; and therein I rejoice" (vs. 18). So, Paul's enemies were abusing the Gospel; preaching only to try to miff the great apostle, but their abuse of the Gospel in no way negates it.

Before the end of the Apostolic Age there were "certain men crept in unawares...ungodly men, turning the grace of our God into lasciviousness, and denying the only Lord God, and our Lord Jesus Christ" (Jude 4). So, grace itself can be perverted. Do we deny grace because of that?

During the Middle Ages, many heretical sects practiced the socialist notions of Plato's *Republic*. For example, the Dulcinian Movement in 13th century Italy believed in holding all things in common, including spouses. This notion came out of their belief in an egalitarian society in which all property was to be held in common. This is a perversion of the example of the early church's practice of holding things like property and money in common (Acts 2:44 & 45). Do we reject entirely the early church because the Dulcinian abuse of her example?

During the Reformation, there were many abuses. For example, in 1534 radical Anabaptists took control of Munster, Germany and established a kind of Christian communist regime. John of Leiden assumed leadership of the movement. He received a vision that polygamy was now permissible. He took sixteen wives for himself.

He reportedly even had a woman beheaded who refused to become part of his harem. The Roman Catholic authorities suppressed the rebellion after a year-long siege in which thousands died. There were other revolts and rebellions by radical Christian groups during this period. Do we reject the entire Protestant Reformation because of these abuses?

In every age there have been improper practices and overzealous, malicious, or deceived Christians who have brought disrepute on Christianity. Hence, we ought not be surprised that spiritual gifts would also be misused in our day. So, the cessationists are really riding a "hobby horse." There is nothing in scripture that refutes the permanence of spiritual gifts, accept for a single verse in I Corinthians (13:8) that is rather speciously interpreted by our cessationist friends.

II. Israel And The Church: Did God Say *Lehitra'ot* To Israel?

Introduction

Lehitra'ot means "farewell" in Hebrew. Did God say farewell to His people after the destruction of the Temple, the Holy City, and the land of Israel in the 1st and 2nd centuries AD by Roman legions? Is this destruction evidence that God had cast off who had once been His people? Are the persecutions Jews have suffered historically proof that God no longer considers them His Chosen People?

Did the iniquities of the Jews merit their divine rejection? Or perhaps their rejection of Jesus of Nazareth as Messiah? Are such questions relevant?

Furthermore, has the church (the body of Christ) replaced Israel? Does the modern State of Israel fulfill Bible prophecy? Do Jews still have a right to the territory that had been promised to their father Abraham and to his descendants? Does it matter whether or not some, or even the majority of Jews returned to the land of their ancestors in "unbelief" in modern times?

Should we be concerned that an organization based on secular-humanism (the United Nations) had such prominence in the establishment of the modern State of

31

Israel? In other words, does the UN imprimatur negate the legitimacy of the modern Jewish state?

These and other questions concerning Israel and the relationship of that nation to the church we will attempt to answer here. This discussion will rely on both history and the Bible, but the Bible will be seen as the primary document of record here.

God's Promises to Abraham

The history of Israel dates from the promises given by God to Abraham, that he would make of the patriarch's descendants a great nation. God told Abram, as he was then called, to leave his country (the land of Padan-Aram), kindred, and home to a land that He would show to him (Gen. 12:1), and He made the following declaration: "I will make of thee a great nation, and I will bless thee, and make thy name great; and thou shalt be a blessing" (Gen. 12:2). It is important to remember that God promised to bless those who blessed him, and to curse those who cursed him (vs. 3).

Abram made his way to the land of Canaan, and on a prominent point overlooking this country , God gave to him this promise: "For all the land thou seest, to thee will I give it, *and to thy seed for ever*" (Gen. 15:15, emphasis added). These italicized words are important to keep in mind.

This divine promise was reiterated to Abram later (Gen. 17) when the patriarch's name would be changed to Abraham ("father of nations," vs. 5). Circumcision was enjoined upon the patriarch and all of his descendants, and they would inherit the land of Canaan *for an everlasting possession* (Gen. 17:8).

Abraham had two sons, Ishmael and Isaac. Although God promised Abraham that Ishmael would become a great nation (Gen. 21:13), the promise would pass to Isaac, because God said this: "For in Isaac shall thy seed by called' (vs. 13).

Isaac had twin boys, Jacob and Esau. Though Esau actually came out of the womb first, and was entitled to the Abrahamic promise, the LORD told Isaac's wife Rebekah that "the elder shall serve the younger" (Gen. 25:23). Esau despised that birthright and the promise passed to Jacob (Gen. 25:29-34). Jacob would have 12 sons, who became the ancestors of the 12 tribes of the nation of Israel. Jacob's name was changed to Israel after he received God's blessing at Peniel (Gen. 32:24-30). Israel became the name collectively for the entire nation later.

So, it is evident that the Creator of the universe gave the land of Canaan to Abraham and his descendants as an everlasting possession. However, were there strings attached to this promised possession?

The Mosaic Covenant

Israel and his sons settled in Egypt to escape a famine in Canaan (Gen. 46:3 & 4). Over the some four-hundred years of the Israelite sojourn in the land of the Nile, they were enslaved by the Egyptians. How that came about is a complicated story. Through putting Israelites in debt, by coercion, by law, or through corruption, the children of Abraham found themselves enslaved en masse sometime during the four-hundred year period, and the oppression by Egyptian Pharaohs and his overlords became worse.

About 1450 BC the Israelites were led out of Egypt by Moses. He mediated the giving of the Law at Mt. Sinai (Ex. 20). It was this Law (and that of all the other ordinances found in the Pentateuch), that would become the basis of moral, civil, and religious life for the Israelite nation.

The story of Balaam illustrates the Abrahamic blessing (Numbers chaps 22-24). This pagan prophet was hired by

Balak king of Moab to curse the people of Israel. He sent a delegation of his elders to hire the false prophet and to accompany them. However, God instructed Balaam: "Thou shalt not go with them; thou shalt not curse the people: for they are blessed" (Numbers 22:12). So, Balaam refused the offer and did not go with them.

In spite of Balaam's refusal of the Moabite king's offer, Balak sent another delegation of even more honorable men. This time God allowed Balaam to accompany them. However, as Balaam rode his donkey through a vineyard, an angel armed with a great sword barred the path. The donkey saw this angel before Balaam had, and the beast baulked and injured the prophet. He struck the donkey, but "the dumb ass speaking with man's voice forbad the madness of the prophet" (II Pet. 2:16). After the LORD opened the eyes of Balaam, the angel of the LORD said to him, "Go with the men: but only the word that I shall speak unto thee, that shalt thou speak" (Num. 22:35).

And so it was. Balak and Balaam went to a high place overlooking the camp of the Israelites. Seven altars were built and a bullock and a ram were offered on each altar.

But, when Balak insisted Balaam curse the sons of Jacob (Num. 23:7), the prophet replied. "How shall I curse, whom God hath not cursed? or shall I defy, *whom* the LORD hath not defied" (vs. 8).

Frustrated, Balak said, "Neither curse them at all, nor bless them at all" (Num. 23:25). Balaam answered that he could speak only what the LORD had told him (vs. 26).

Balak brought Balaam to the top of a Mount Peor. Seven more altars were built, and a bullock and a ram offered upon each as before. As Balaam gazed upon the tents of Israel in the valley below, he began to prophesy in most flowery verse: "How goodly are thy tents O Jacob, and thy tabernacles, O Israel" (Num. 24:5). He ended his prophecy with these words: "Blessed *is* he that blesseth thee, and cursed *is* he that curseth thee" (vs. 9), reiterating the words of God's promise to Abraham.

Balak insisted again, that Balaam curse Israel. Instead, he prophesied the coming of Messiah: "There shall come a Star out of Jacob, and a Sceptre shall rise out of Israel" (Num. 24;17).

After prophesying the destruction of Israel's enemies, Balaam returned to his home and Balak also went his way (Num. 24:18-25). Balak got nothing for his money and received a lesson that has been repeated throughout history. Curses upon Israel are turned to blessing, and those who bless Israel will received a blessing. Balaam stirred up the Midianites against the tribes of Israel, and he was killed in the battle that followed, receiving the just recompense for his folly (Num. 31:8; Jude 11).

The Deuteronomic Code seems to indicate the blessing on Israel is conditional upon the keeping of the Law (Deut. 28:1-14). Breaking the Law would incur the wrath of God, including both the carrying away of the people from the Promised Land to a foreign country, and loss of the land (vss. 36 & 37). However, this is a cursory reading of the Scriptures only. The Jewish people hold the title deed to the land *in perpetuity*.

Under Joshua the Israelites finally realized the Abrahamic Promise of receiving the land of Canaan. The land was secured under this conquering chief. He divided the land of Canaan by lot, with each tribe receiving its appointed portion of the country (Joshua, chaps. 13-21).

The Land Lost, Regained, Lost, and Regained

The conquest of Canaan gave the Israelites a land of milk and honey (Lev. 20:24). It was a land of gentle rain, wheat, and barley; a land of figs, grapes, and pomegranates. Of course, often, the description of the Promised Land is idealized. Nonetheless, it was a place that early on became beloved of the people of Israel. (Josh. 14:12).

Around 1400 BC the Israelites conquered most of the land of Canaan. They began to develop the country and put an Israelite stamp on the place. The Israelites were not many years from the idolatry of Egypt at this time. In fact, the Israelites had hardly escaped from the bondage (both spiritually and physically) of Egypt when they made a golden-calf idol and began to worship it in the absence of the leadership of Moses, who had been fasting on the Mount of God waiting to receive the Ten Commandments (Ex. 32). The image of a calf with a sun disk between its horns was a principal idol of the Egyptians.

The Canaanites were steeped in idolatry. They had a high god El, but the most prominent god of these peoples was the storm deity Baal (meaning "owner"). Dagon was another important god, as were goddesses such as Astarte and Anath. Kothar-wa-Hasis was a divine artificer, like the Roman god Vulcan or the Greek god Hephaestus.

The Canaanites and Amorites were not only idolaters, but their religious practices were of a type far more depraved than that seen in Egypt. The Israelites participated in these practices, which included human sacrifice (II Ki. 23:4-15). They either forsook the worship of Yahweh altogether, or "mixed and matched" the worship of the God of Israel with the idolatry of their Canaanite neighbors, even in the Temple itself (Ezek. 8).

The prophets spoke against this situation and warned the people of the consequences of violating the 1st and 2nd Commandments of the Decalogue (II Ki. 17; Ezra 9; Neh. 9; Ezek. 20; 22 & 23). The Israelites would be judged by being carried away captive into foreign lands (Deut. 28:49, 64; 29:28; Lev. 25:5 & 6; Mic. 4:10; Hab. 1:12-17).

The Northern Kingdom of Israel was idolatrous from its founding (I Ki. 12:25-13:1). It was warned repeatedly by prophets like Elijah and Elisha and was finally carried away captive by the Assyrians in 722 BC. The kingdom of Judah, unlike Israel, had a few decent kings, nonetheless, she too was carried away captive after the destruction of Jerusalem in 587 BC by the Babylonians.

However, Isaiah prophesied the rebuilding of both the Holy City and the Temple under a ruler by the name of Cyrus (4:28). This was *one hundred and fifty years* before the Persian monarch made the decree. Jeremiah prophesied a period of 70 years' captivity (25:8-14; 29:10-14). The three deportations are summarized in Jer. 52:28-30: 3,023 Jews carried away into exile in the first deportation; 745 taken in the second deportation; and 4,600 carried away in the third deportation. These were largely members of the noble families and craftsmen.

Daniel in the first year of Persian king Darius surmised from reading Jeremiah that the exile of Judah and the desolations of Jerusalem were coming to an end. In 538 BC Cyrus allowed the Jewish people to return to their land and even supplied funds for doing so. Between 521-516 BC the Second Temple was reconstructed.

The return of the Jewish nation to the land was also according to promise. In the Mosaic covenant the relationship between the people and the land is directly related to their spiritual status before God. So, any separation of Israel from the land would be followed by a return of the people according to the sovereignty of God (Lev. 26:40-45):

> "And yet for all that, when they be in the land of their enemies, I will not cast them away, neither will I abhor them, to destroy them utterly, and to break my covenant with them: for I am the LORD their God" (vs. 44).

So, it would seem that the promise of restoration is repeatedly expounded upon in scripture. It is often stated that the Lord will "bring back the captivity of Zion" (Ps. 126:1) and that He would "restore the fortunes of Jacob" (Isa. 49:5; Nahum 2:2).

This is reiterated in the New Testament. Jesus specifically mentions a restored Israel (Mt. 19:28), as does Peter in Acts 3:21. In Romans, Paul specifically declares that "God hath not cast away his people which he foreknew" (11:2).

Even concerted efforts to thwart the Abrahamic Promise did not cause the Jewish people to give up hope. After the Bar Kochba revolt (132-135 AD) the Romans changed the name of Judea to Palestina, after the country of the Philistines, the inveterate enemies of Israel. Jerusalem was renamed Aeolia Capitolina, after the name of the family of Roman Emperor Hadrian. A temple to Jupiter was built on the Temple Mount. Jews were forbidden by pain of death from living in or even visiting the Holy City.

Jerusalem was captured by Arab Caliph Omar in 638 AD, and in 691 a mosque called the Dome of the Rock was built on the site of the destroyed Jewish Temple. The Arabs called Jerusalem "Al Quds" ("The Holy"). The city and land would remain under Muslim rule, accept when it was under Crusader control (1099-1187 and 1229-1244), until 1917 when the British took Jerusalem during World War I.

41

The British capture of Jerusalem coincided with the Balfour Declaration. The history of this declaration begins with Britain's declaration of war against the Ottoman Empire in November of 1914. Within a couple months a memorandum was presented to the War Cabinet by Herbert Samuel, who was also a *Zionist*. He proposed securing the worldwide support of Jews in the Allied effort by proposing the creation of a Jewish homeland in Palestine. His proposal was considered and finally authorized following the British victory at the Battle of Beersheba in southern Palestine on Oct. 31, 1917. It was determined that this victory gave the British immense propaganda value amongst the worldwide Jewish community for the Allied cause. The declaration was issued as part of a letter dated Nov. 2, 1917 from British Foreign Secretary Arthur Balfour to Lord Rothschild for distribution to the Zionist Federation of Great Britain and Ireland. The text of the declaration was delivered to the press on Nov. 9, 1917.

So, for Jews living between 135-1917 it seemed a forlorn hope that they would ever have a country of their own. Now there was a glimmer of hope of a return to the Promised Land. Nevertheless, every Shabbat they continued to pray, "Next year in Jerusalem."

During the years of the British mandate, Jews began to move back to the Holy Land. Arab Muslims began to resist this movement early on. In 1929 a Palestinian Arab mob killed 133 Jews and injured another 339. However, even this resistance did not keep Jews from returning to the land, or making *aliyah*. This accelerated especially after the *anti-Semitic* Nazi regime came to power in Germany in 1933.

World War II saw the systematic destruction of the Jews of Europe. About six million Jews were killed, as were an equal number of others considered enemies by the authorities of Hitler's Third Reich. Many of the Jewish survivors of the death camps attempted to make their way to Palestine. However, to appease the Arabs, the British mandatory authorities attempted to prevent this latter-day Exodus. As a consequence, Palestinian Jews began to resist, organizing guerrilla groups like the Haganah, Irgun, and the Stern Group. We must add, the main resistance group, the Haganah, was defensive only and mainly existed to smuggle Jewish refugees into Palestine.

On Nov. 29, 1947 the United Nations adopted Resolution 181, which both ended the British mandate and partitioned Palestine into Jewish and Arab states in May 1948. The Jews accepted the partition plan, but the Arabs rejected it, and showed their displeasure by doing what they always had done, by attacking and murdering Jewish civilians.

On May 14, 1948 Prime Minister David Ben-Gurion declared the independence of the Jewish portion of the partitioned country. He declared that the policy of the new State of Israel would be equal rights for all Israeli citizens whether Arab, Christian, or Jew. However, almost immediately Egypt, Jordan, Syria, Iraq, and Lebanon began military operations against the new nation. Though outnumbered and outgunned, Israel emerged victorious. In fact, the nature of Israel's victory could only be called miraculous.

The newly formed IDF numbered about 60,000. However only about 22,000 were armed with firearms, and a smaller number of them had modern military small arms. They had no tanks, no combat aircraft, no navy, and only 8 obsolete artillery pieces that could be described as museum quality at best.

They faced Arab armies about double their number armed with tanks, artillery, combat aircraft, and naval units. Additionally, thousands of well-armed irregulars operated as guerilla formations, concentrating most of their attacks against Jewish civilians in rear areas.

The Arab armies eventually became bogged down, and as more military equipment began to reach the Israeli Defense Force (IDF), this ragtag Jewish army won territory greater than that assigned by the UN partition,

There is no injustice against the Arab Palestinians in this. If you start a war and lose it, you can't object if you lose territory.

The Palestinians heeded the wrong-headed advice of Arab political and religious leaders who broadcast instructions to leave their homes and seek refuge in Arab lands. They were promised that victorious Arab armies would soon drive every Jew into the sea. So, this was essentially to be a war of extermination, a continuation of the policy of the Nazis.

A tenuous cease-fire was brokered by the UN in 1949. For the first time in two-thousand years, Jews were in charge of their own nation, and it was, indeed, a fulfillment of Old Testament prophecy, as we have already seen, and will explain further in the next section.

The Jews are a Sign of God's Faithfulness

Hatred of God's chosen people did not begin with the Nazis. It has manifested itself throughout history. The first attempt to destroy them was initiated by the Pharaoh of Egypt. Famine drove the patriarch Israel, his sons, and their families to take refuge in the land of the Nile. There they "were fruitful, and increased abundantly, and multiplied, and waxed exceeding mighty; and the land was filled with them" (Ex. 1:7). Within a few hundred years, the Egyptians began to fear this vast host would ally with an invader. Therefore, the Egyptian monarch ordered all midwives to destroy the male babies born of the Israelites. "But the midwives feared God, and did not as the king of Egypt commanded them, but saved the men children alive" (vs. 18).

During the reign of Xerxes, king of Persia, a powerful and evil man by the name of Haman the Agagite connived to destroy all the Jews of the land in order to avenge a personal slight by the king's Jewish gatekeeper by the name of Mordecai. This plan was frustrated by the bravery of the Persian king's Jewish wife Esther, who pleaded the cause of her people before her royal husband and exposed the knavery of Haman at the same time. The tables were turned on Haman and on all the enemies of the Jews in Persia. The Jewish feast of Purim celebrates this deliverance (see the Book of Esther).

Seleucid king Antiochus Epiphanes (c.215-164 B.C.) was enraged both by his defeat in Egypt, and because Menelaus, his chosen high priest in Jerusalem, had been overthrown by a man called Jason. On his return from Egypt, he attacked Jerusalem:

> "Raging like a wild animal, he set out from
> Egypt and took Jerusalem by storm. He
> ordered his soldiers to cut down without
> mercy those who they met and to slay

those who took refuge in their houses. There was a massacre of young and old, killing of women and children, a slaughter of virgins and infants. In the space of three days eighty thousand were lost, forty thousand by slaughter, and the same number sold into slavery" (II Macc. 5:11-14).

Antiochus tried to suppress the worship of Jehovah and substitute the worship of the Greek god Zeus. This was resisted by a Levite by the name of Mattathias the Hasmonean. He and his sons led an army against the forces of Antiochus and the apostate Jews who collaborated with him. Mattathias was killed in battle, and his son Judas Maccabeus continued the struggle against the policy of Helenization, i.e., the forcing of Jews to become cultural and religious Greeks. This struggle was a success, and Israel achieved its independence for over a century (140-37 B.C.).

Under the Romans, the Jews suffered terribly. During the First Jewish Revolt (66-73 A.D.), about 1.1 million non-combatants died in Jerusalem, and another 97,000 Jews were carried off into slavery (Josephus, *Wars of the Jews*, VI, 9.3).

It is estimated that 580,000 Jews died at the hands of the Romans as a result of the Bar Kochba Revolt (132-135 B.C.). Jerusalem itself was renamed Aelia Capitolina, and Jews were forbidden on pain of death to enter within the walls of the city. Judea was renamed as well, designated for the first time after the country of the Philistines-- Palestina or *Palestine*.

During the Middle Ages, both the Roman Catholic Church and Islam persecuted the Jews.

The papal Inquisition was first established by Pope Gregory IX in 1233 to combat the *Albigenses*. However, the Inquisition was also used to bring charges against Jews.

One of the most scandalous accusations brought against the Jews was that of *blood-libel*. Blood-libel is still declared to be a fact in parts of the Muslim world and is still believed by some in backward areas of Russia and elsewhere. This insidious slander accuses Jews of kidnapping and killing Christian children in order to mix their blood with the Passover matzoth. The charge is patently false, because Jews are forbidden to consume blood (Gen. 9:4; Lev. 3:17; 17:10, 12 & 13; Deut. 12:16, 24; I Sam.14:33 & 34).

Jewish scholars were ordered by European nobles to debate with Roman Catholic scholars. The Jew would invariably lose the disputation and would be imprisoned. The Jews of the realm could be collectively fined, expelled from the region, or have their synagogues sacked or burned.

Muhammed, the founder of Islam, began persecuting the Jews of Yathrib (Medina) after only a few of them converted to Islam. Since he was not Jewish, they would not accept his claim to being a prophet. Thereafter, Muhammed began to expunge Jewish influence from Islam. He shifted the *qiblah*, or the direction Muslims face while in prayer from Jerusalem to Mecca. He declared Friday to be the day of special prayer, rather than the Jewish Shabbat. All Jewish dietary laws except the prohibition against eating pork, were renounced. Furthermore, he began to deny the connection of the Jews to the prophet Abraham.

Muhammed expelled two Jewish tribes from Medina and murdered 600 male members of a third tribe and sold the women and children into slavery.

The Quran has many verses that condemn Christians, idolaters, and especially Jews. The following surat (chapters) of the Quran reveal this fact:

The Surah of the Cow:

2:88: And they say: "Our hearts are covered." Nay, Allah has cursed them on account of their unbelief; so little it is they believe.

2:111: And they say: "None shall enter paradise except he who is a Jew or a Christian." These are their vain desires. Answer them: "Bring evidence if you are truthful."

2:135: And they say: "Be Jews or Christians, you will be on the right path." Answer them: "Nay! We follow the religion of Ibrahim the Hanif, and he was not one of the polytheists."

The Surah of the Table Spread

5:51: O you who believe! Do not take the Jews or the Christians for your friends.

5:64: And the Jews say: "The hand of Allah is tied!" Their hands shall be shackled and they shall be cursed for what they say.

5:78: Those who disbelieved from among the children of Israel were cursed by the tongue of Dawood and Isa, son of Mariam. (That is, David and Jesus Son of Mary).

The Hadith of Al-Burkhari is also a source of Muslim anti-Jewish sentiment:

Vol. 4, 56. 791: I heard the messenger of Allah say, "The Jews will fight you, and you will be given victory over them so that a stone will say, "O Muslim! There is a Jew behind me; kill him."

Similar calls to dispatch Jews are repeated in other verses of the Hadith (Vol. 4, 52, 176; 52, 177; Sahih Book 041, 6981, 6983, etc.). These verses are in the charter of the terrorist group Hamas, which until recently ran the Gaza Strip with an iron first. This terror group is a direct link to the Grand Mufti of Jerusalem, Haj Amin al-Husseini (1897-1974). This man was a notorious sympathizer with Nazism and faithfully served the Third Reich right up until its inglorious end.

Husseini delivered a speech at an Arab political conference in Syria in September of 1937. In 1938 the Nazi press translated the speech into German. This speech was circulated all over the Arab world and has become a source of anti-Semitism to this day.

The Nazis helped fund Husseini's 1936-1939 Palestinian revolt. Hundreds of British soldiers, Jews, and moderate Arabs were killed by his thugs. He attempted to arrange a pro-fascist coup in Iraq in 1941. The coup attempt failed, so he fled to Berlin where he was received as Hitler's personal guest.

Between 1941-1945 Husseini aided the Nazis in other ways. He broadcast Nazi propaganda to the Middle East by radio during the period. He also helped organize a Bosnian Muslim 13th SS Mountain Division, a unit which committed hundreds of atrocities in Yugoslavia against Jews, Serbs, Gypsies, and others.

Husseini escaped to Egypt in 1946, and while there was instrumental in pushing the Arabs to reject the 1947 United Nations plan that would have peacefully partitioned Palestine into Jewish and Arab states. Instead, he advocated a "war of destruction." Hence, had the Arab invasion of Israel in 1948 succeeded, it would have led to a second Holocaust.

The Grand Mufti's marriage of Nazism's genocidal Jew-hatred with Islam has become a hallmark of Islamism worldwide and has inspired the following terrorist organizations: the PLO (under Yasser Arafat), Hamas, Islamic Jihad, Hezbollah, al-Qaeda, ISIS, etc. Hezbollah terrorists still use the stiff-armed Nazi salute in their parades to this day. The Grand Mufti also inspired Iran's Ayatollah Khomeini, who would tune in to Radio Berlin every evening to hear the venomous pro-Nazi broadcasts of the Palestinian cleric.

So, in a deep sense, Nazism did not die in the ruins of Berlin in 1945. The ideology still has a host of followers today. If another monster like Hitler would somehow arise in Europe or somewhere else today, is there any doubt he would be well received in the Middle East?

Holding to "replacement theology" and believing government social programs are equivalent to Christian charity, Liberal denominations in Germany tended to back Nazism.

Replacement theology states that when Israel rejected Jesus as her Messiah, God irrevocably rejected that nation and set up the Gentile Church as the New Israel. Hence, all the blessings in the Bible that once applied to Israel, now apply to the church.

However, what does the Apostle Paul tell us in Romans 11:1: "Hath God cast away his people? God forbid" (or, "May it never be!"). . . . God hath not cast away his people which he foreknew" (vs. 2). The apostle explains further that Israel's hardness concerning the fact that Jesus is the Messiah will continue until "the fulness of the Gentiles be come in" (vs. 25). What exactly this entails is not quite clear at the present. But what we *can* say for sure is this: God has by no means irrevocably rejected Israel: "For the gifts and calling of God are without repentance" (vs. 29).

To dispel this notion that God has rejected His people it will be necessary to quote at length a passage from the Psalms (105:6-11):

> "O ye seed of Abraham his servant, ye children of Jacob his chosen. He is the LORD our God: his judgments are in all the earth. He hath remembered his covenant for ever, the word which he commanded to a thousand generations. Which covenant he made with Abraham, and his oath unto Isaac; And confirmed the same unto Jacob for a law, and to Israel for an everlasting covenant: Saying, Unto thee will I give the land of
>
> Canaan, the lot of your inheritance."

God's faithfulness to Israel is not based on Israel's faithfulness to Him. God says "they may forget, yet will I not forget thee" (Isa. 49:15).

The very next verse in Isaiah also declares this: "Behold, I have graven thee upon the palms of my hands; thy walls are continually before me." This is speaking of Zion, but as a metonymy of the whole nation of Israel, the verse is making it plain that God will not cast off the people whom He has chosen.

The clincher, however, is from the prophet Jeremiah (30:35 & 36). He excoriated Israel, but informs us that God's covenant with that nation is *permanent*:

> "Thus saith the LORD, which giveth the sun for a light by day, and the ordinances of the moon and of the stars for a light by night, which divideth the sea when the waves thereof roar; the LORD of hosts is his name: If those ordinances depart from before me, saith the LORD, *then* the seed of Israel also shall cease from being a nation before me for ever."

So Biblical justification for Jew-hatred cannot stand, unless one cherry-picks verses out of context. Hence, the most effective antidote to the kind of anti-Semitism advocated by Nazis, Islamists, Black Muslims, White Supremacists, and other miscreants is an appeal to

Scripture, and its sub theme of God's faithfulness to His people after the flesh, Israel..

Conclusion

When Fredrick the Great of Prussia asked a Lutheran pastor a proof for God's existence, the pastor answered, "The Jews." The mere survival of this people is so obviously the result of God's providential protection that His existence really cannot be denied.

Israel not only offers proof of God's existence, but this nation has also been recognized as a kind of moral conscience of the world. Did a great Jewish sage or rabbi say this? In a round about way perhaps, but it was Adolf Hitler who actually stated it in so many words. He unequivocally declared the conscience to be a Jewish invention, and for Hitler a moral conscience was a hindrance to the emergence of the *ubermensch*, the superior human untrammeled by scruples and morals.

Abraham is the proto-type Jew. As forebear of the Jewish people he was called a *Hebrew*. He was a Hebrew because he was from "the other side of the river" (i.e., the Euphrates) *ever hanahar*. Abraham came from the other side of the Euphrates, a land of pagan darkness, to trod a land that would become a great nation. He took with him the light of ethical monotheism and its moral clarity. This moral clarity he passed on to his descendants, and from his descendants, to the rest of the world.

Moreover, we have Israel to thank for the scriptures, as the Apostle Paul tells us, "Unto them were committed the oracles of God" (Rom. 3:2). The Word of God has transformed not just individuals, but whole societies. Modern concepts of individual rights and freedoms ultimately come from the Bible (Lev. 25:10; Isa. 61:1; Jer. 34:8; Lk. 4:8; II Cor. 3:17; Gal. 5:1). We have the nation of Israel to thank for this as well.

Finally, as Jesus said to the Samaritan woman, "Ye worship ye know not what: we know what we worship: for salvation is from the Jews" (Jn. 4:22), and since "faith *cometh* by hearing, and hearing by the word of God" (Rom. 10:17); we can conclude that the Jewish scriptures, including the New Testament, are an instrument of salvation. However, salvation is dependent, not only on the writings of scripture, but ultimately upon a man who was born, lived, and died a Jew, the Lord Jesus Christ.

Jesus was born of a virgin and raised as a Jew. He was born in a Jewish village (Mt. 1:18-25; Lk. 2:1-7), circumcised according to Jewish Law (Gen. 17:12; Lev. 12:3; Lk. 2:21-38), raised in a northern Israelite town (Mt.

2:13), attended Passover in Jerusalem (Lk.2:41 & 42), and attended and even taught in Jewish synagogues (Mt. 12:9; Lk. 4:16; Jn. 6:59; 18:20). However, as a Jew He was both mortal flesh, but also God of the universe (Jn. 1:1). As perfect man, He could represent sinful humanity to God; as Deity, He could represent God to humanity.

As "the Lamb of God which taketh away the sin of the world" (Jn. 1:29), Jesus is God's gift to mankind. However, that gift was wrapped in the wrapping paper of Judaism, so in a real sense Jesus is also Israel's gift to humanity. So, considering the many blessings Israel has given to the world, and the Ultimate Gift of God's Son, it would seem the Jews deserve a small slice of land of their own and to be left in peace. Perhaps, if this people on their small plot of territory are left to develop it, the world at large may learn to live in peace with one another.

III. The New Atheists: How Do We Answer Them According To The Bible and Logic?

Introduction

The following are the prominent New Atheists: Richard Dawkins, Sam Harris, Daniel Dennett, and the late Christopher Hitchens. They have been termed "the four horsemen," and are far more militant in their atheism than atheists have been previously, such that they have been termed "evangelists for atheism." The New Atheists are advocates of confronting religion as superstition and, as such, roundly denounce it as irrational. Moreover, they assert that when religious belief exerts undue influence on society at large, especially on education and politics, it should be especially criticized and challenged.

Dawkins made this observation when he wrote, "I don't object to the horseman label, by the way, I'm less keen on 'new atheist': it isn't clear to me how we differ from old atheists" (pg. 15).

A *secular humanist* named Paul Kurtz (1929-2012) is often considered the predecessor of New Atheism. However, it was probably the terror attacks of Sep. 11, 2001 that boosted the popularity of New Atheist authors. In fact, Sam Harris not only blamed Islam, but also criticized Judaism and Christianity, as well (see *The End of Faith: Religion, Terror and the Future of Reason,* 2004).

Hitchens authored his own screed entitled *God Is Not Great* in 2007. In addition to his writings (*Darwin's Dangerous Idea* and *Breaking the Spell*), Dennett supports apostate clergy who are fearful of losing their livelihood by announcing to their congregations they can no longer believe in God. Dennett's counsel to them was a deceptive "just don't tell 'em" policy, since such an announcement would mean the loss of employment and parsonage.

Another key figure in the New Atheist movement was Ayaan Hirsi Ali. Hirsi Ali was born in Somalia, but fled there to the Netherlands in 1992 to escape an arranged marriage. She became involved in Dutch politics and rejected her former Muslim faith. In 2012 she appeared with Dawkins, Harris, and Dennett at a worldwide atheist confab, where she was dubbed by her atheist colleagues the "Fifth Horseman" (Blumner, Dec. 2020).

However, Hirsi Ali became involved with Islamic critic Theo van Gogh and his film *Submission*, writing the screenplay. *Submission* was an expose of Islam's treatment of women, informing its audience of barbaric practices like clitoridectomy and child betrothal.

Van Gogh was stabbed to death by a Muslim extremist, who penned to his murder victim's chest a note with a death threat to Hirsi Ali. She went into hiding and later traveled to the United States, where she remains a staunch critic of Islam. Ali announced in a column in November of 2023 that she had converted to

Christianity, declaring the Judeo-Christian tradition is the only answer for the problems of today's world. In that, we would concur.

Score one for the good guys.

Answering Atheists New and Old

Actually, though our New Atheists have been effective media hounds, their objections to theism are really no better than their unbelieving forebears. Jonathon Sacks makes the following observation about Christopher Hitchens and company:

> "Atheism deserves better than the new atheists whose methodology consists of criticizing religion without understanding it, quoting texts without contexts, taking exceptions to the rule, confusing folk belief with reflective theology, abusing, mocking, ridiculing, caricaturing, and demonizing religious faith and holding it responsible for the great crimes against humanity. Religion has done harm; I acknowledge that. But the cure for bad religion is good religion, not no religion, just as the cure for bad science is good

science, not the abandonment of science"
(pg. 11).

So, we counter the New Atheists just as we do the Old Atheists, with proofs for the existence of a Supreme Being. As clever as some of their quips might be, the ridicule of the New Atheists are neither good arguments nor evidence that belief in the Creator is a figment of the imagination..

Atheism Represents An Inadequate Worldview

As we begin our critique of atheism, we ought first to examine it as a *worldview*. A proper worldview "must be able to answer four questions: that of origin, meaning of life, morality, and destiny" (Zacharias, Ravi; quoted in Stroud, pg. 23).

Theism, that is "belief-in-Godism," posits as an absolute fundamental fact the existence of a personal, all-knowing (omniscient), all-powerful (omnipotent), transcendent, moral, infinite Creator of the universe. Additionally, this Creator-God sustains the universe by establishing natural laws that govern it, but is not Himself bound by those laws.

Atheism, or "there-is-no-Godism," is a belief that there is no Supreme Being, spirit, or soul; that the physical universe is all there is, a philosophy based on *materialism*.

There is no basis for morality in the atheistic worldview. If there is no God who reveals Himself as a moral Lawgiver, then there is no real basis for morality.

However, the New Atheists give the following arguments for morality apart from the existence of a Supreme Being:

(1) It evolved as a means of survival within groups, so that morality provided an advantage for right behavior.

(2) *Utilitarianism* offers some atheists and other unbelievers an answer for morality, that it maximizes the happiness for the greatest number of persons.

(3) Human reason is emphasized by other atheists, who believe morality is obvious to anyone who uses critical thinking to solve ethical dilemmas.

(4) Many atheists, both New and Old, are committed to *secular humanism*, a philosophy that promotes moral and ethical behavior.

C. S. Lewis summarized why moral arguments indicate a moral God (Geisler, pg. 500):

(1) Divine moral law must exist universally, or: (a) moral disagreements would be without basis, and we all assume they have a basis, (b) there would be no basis for moral criticisms, (c) promises to keep contracts or even international treaties would be optional, and it is assumed when these agreements were made that this is not the case, and (d) why do human beings make excuses for themselves when they violate moral law, a thing everyone does.

(2) The Source of a universal moral law must require a Moral Lawgiver because (a) the Source declares moral precepts, and (b) the Source is concerned with our moral behavior.

(3) Furthermore, a universal Moral Lawgiver would of necessity be absolutely good: (a) else all moral activity would be pointless, and we would be denying ourselves (our passions, desires, greeds, etc.) for no good reason, and (b) the Source of all good must be absolutely good, since ultimately the standard of all good must be completely good.

(4) Therefore, there must exist an absolutely good Moral Lawgiver.

In theology, this is called the *moral argument* for the existence of God.

Atheism is an inadequate worldview because it has no real answer for the origin of things. Atheists believe they have a logical answer to the problem of origins. According to the First Law of Thermodynamics, energy can neither be created nor destroyed, so the universe is eternal, therefore, it needs no Creator.

However, an eternal universe would of necessity imply an infinite series of events. And an infinite series of events could have no beginning since an attempt to get back to the beginning of the infinite series would involve an infinite number of moments and it would always be possible to add one more moment to the series. But one more number cannot be added to or subtracted from infinity. Since we have reached today, it is evident that a finite number of moments have been traversed. Therefore, the universe is not eternal. It had to have had a beginning. That which had begun the beginning had to have been more powerful than the universe itself, and we recognize that as the Creator (*ibid.*, pg. 366).

In theology, this is called the *cosmological argument* for the existence of God.

Atheism and the theory of evolution are wedded. This theory was first made widely known and was accepted, especially in academic circles, by the publication of *The Origin of Species* by Charles Darwin in 1859. Darwin speculated that life began in a "warm little pond." Taking this cue, researchers have shown that it is possible to produce organic compounds in the "warm little pond" of a laboratory.

In 1953 Dr. Harold Urey wanted to confirm speculation about how life could have been formed from the earth's primeval sea. He put a graduate student by the name of Stanley Miller to work on the problem. In a sealed system of flasks he placed methane, ammonia, hydrogen, and water vapor and subjected the mixture to an electrical charge of 60,000 volts to simulate lightning. After a week, a collection flask at the end of the system was filled with water that had turned a deep red. An analysis of this liquid showed it to contain a number of amino acids--the very building blocks of life! (Warshofsky, p. 140). This experiment proved organic compounds could be made by artificial means, but does it also prove that life could have arisen in a lifeless primitive ocean from raw chemicals and a jolt of electrical energy?

This experiment is unrealistic for the following reasons (Huse, pp. 154-156):

1. There is no evidence to suggest the earth's early atmosphere was a reducing atmosphere of methane and ammonia.

2. There *is* evidence to show the earth has always had an oxidizing atmosphere (one containing oxygen), and oxygen would have been fatal to the Urey-Miller experiment.

3. Methane and ammonia were carefully chosen because it was known that these would produce organic compounds. Hence, Miller and Urey "stacked the deck" to get the outcome they desired.

4. A reducing atmosphere of methane and ammonia would have been fatal to life forms.

5. An actual lightning strike would have destroyed any life forms.

Furthermore, it is universally recognized that life never arises from nonlife. Nature can produce organic compounds, but it can never harness the energy to select the right amino acids and to choose those which could build proteins and be enclosed in a cell membrane and the entire thing able to replicate itself. But, as Geisler observes, "It is easy to pump a lot of energy into a system at random to make it hot, but to organize it and create information requires intelligence" (pg. 229). Hence, how ever the first cell was made an intelligent superintending force had to have been present there to bring it about. And if this intelligent superintending force had the ability to create a single living cell, why not an entire array of multi-cellular life forms?

Researchers are no closer to creating a living cell from raw chemicals than they were those many years ago in the lab of Dr. Urey.

Intelligent design is an example of what is called in theology, the *teleological argument* for the existence of God.

The Bible Agrees with Reason

The Scriptures speak of God's absolute moral perfection. The Lord Jesus says this, "Be ye perfect, therefore, as your heavenly Father is perfect" (Mt. 5:48). Again, we are told in Deut. 32:4 "He is the Rock, his work is perfect:

for all his ways are judgment: a God of truth and without iniquity, just and right *is* he."

God's holiness and moral perfection is the basis of His Law (see Ex. 20). He has given this Law to humanity and expects us to live according to its precepts (Deut. 27:26; Gal. 3:10; Jas. 1:25). However, because we are all born with a sin nature and are under its curse (Gen. 5:3; Job 15:14; 25:4; Ps. 51:53; Jn. 8:7; Rom. 3:9; Gal. 3:22), we are under its condemnation (I Cor. 6:9; Gal. 5:19; Eph. 5:5; Rev. 21:27).

That is not the end of the story, however. Since Jesus of Nazareth is without sin (II Cor. 5:21; Heb. 4:15; 7:26; I Jn.3:5), His blood alone redeems us from sin (Zech. 13:1; Jn. 1:29; Eph. 1:7; I Jn. 1:7). Man needs redemption because he has offended a holy God.

The Bible also tells the truth about humanity. The human race is described in the most unflattering terms (Rom. 3:10-18). We cannot say the Bible is "piling on" either. A glance at the local section of any metropolitan newspaper will confirm the Bible's assessment of humanity. Though we heartily disagree with his assessment, one skeptic observed that the doctrine of man's moral depravity is the only Christian doctrine that can be verified empirically. Not even the heroes of the Bible are exempt from having the worst of their foibles and shortcomings recorded. Books written exclusively by men have a tendency to cover up or justify the sins of their heroic individuals.

At one time most astronomers held to a cosmology based on what is called the Steady State Theory. According to this theory, the universe was expanding, but matter was being continually created at all points in space. Observations in the 1960s led to the abandonment of this theory. The Doppler Effect revealed that galaxies were moving away from each other in a phenomenon known as the *Red Shift*. However, the strongest evidence came from a study of background radiation, which showed the temperature of it was 3° above absolute zero Kelvin in all parts of the universe where this radiation could be measured. This would be the heat remaining from the Big Bang.

Although we may object to it, nonetheless, a Big Bang does point to a time when the universe suddenly came into being. We prefer to call this event the Creation, and the Bible tells us this in its first verse: "In the beginning, God created the heaven and the earth." The following verses also indicate that God is the Creator: Deut. 4:19; Neh. 9:6; Job 33:4; 38:4-11; Ps. 8; 19:1; 33:6; 89:11; Isa. 37:16; 40:28; Jer. 10:12; Jn. 1:3; Acts 17:24; Rom. 1:25; Col. 1:26; Heb. 1:10; I Pet. 4:19; Rev. 4:11.

The Bible also indicates that God is the Master Designer: "He that formed the eye, shall he not see?" The eye is an amazing biological "device," such that even Darwin himself was said to feel ill at the mere contemplation of it (Davidheiser, p. 144).

Like a camera, the eye has a diaphragm and variable focusing. This biological device has the ability to make more than 100,000 adjustments in a single day and take a continuous series of stereoscopic pictures in living color.

Read the following description of the molecular mechanism for sight, and try to explain how this could have come about by random chance and natural selection (Behe, pp. 18-

20):

> When light first strikes the retina a photon interacts with a molecule called 11-cis retinal, which rearranges within picoseconds to *trans*retinal. (A picosecond is about the time it takes light to travel the breadth of a single human hair.) The change in the shape of the retinal molecule forces a change in the shape of the protein, rhodopsin, to which the retinal is tightly bound. The protein's

metamorphosis alters its behavior. Now called metarhodopsin II, the protein sticks to another protein, called transducin. Before bumping into metarhodopsin II, transducin had tightly bound a small molecule called GDP. But when transducin interacts with metarhodopsin II, the GDP falls off, and a molecule called GTP binds to transducin. (GTP is closely related to, but critically different from, GDP.)

A Darwinist might answer this by pointing out that the obvious complexity observed in the human eye is a result of *millions of years* of a trial-and-error process guided by gene mutation and *natural selection*. However, complex eyes show up in the fossil record at the very beginning.

The arguments for the existence of God we have reviewed above belong to what is called *natural theology*. Natural theology is that which can be known of God by reason alone by means of *general revelation* (see Rom. 1:19 & 20).

Since arguments for the existence of God have an entirely rational basis, it is evident that belief in a Creator is not on the level of belief in Santa Claus, the Easter Bunny, or the Tooth Fairy, as the New Atheists assert.

Since the Bible is in agreement with the rationality of the existence of a Supreme Being, it therefore speaks volumes about its veracity.

Conclusion

In order for a world view to be true, it must be consistent, i.e., it must meet the coherence test. If any part of it is false, the whole world view must be determined to be false. For example, the secular worldview of the New Atheists cannot be true because it denies that man has a corrupt nature. A corrupt nature would imply a corruption of will, and many, if not most atheists, would deny that human beings even possess such a thing as a free will. A free will is not something that can be measured, weighed, nor does it extend into space. Hence, it is immaterial. It is that part of the mind that makes decisions, but atheists with a materialist worldview also deny the existence of mind, attributing thought entirely to synapses firing in the brain.

The Bible affirms that human beings are possessed of a free will (Jn. 1:13; Rom. 7:18; II Tim. 2:8; Rev. 22:17). This is part of the image of God that man possesses from the creation (Gen. 1:27), because God Himself has a will (Dan. 4:17; Rom. 9:19; Eph. 1:5; .Jas. 1:18). That God would have a free will is also evident from reason.

Also, the New Atheists cannot adequately account for the beginning of the universe, since it is obviously not eternal, it had to have had a Cause more powerful than itself and quite apart from it. This is obvious. The worldview of the New Atheists cannot account for the creation of life either. That life can only come from life is so self evident that to deny it would be to deny reality itself. Life could not have arisen from nonlife because *abiogenesis* is not possible.

The fact that biological systems have purpose is an indication of *design*. The Bible affirms this (Gen. 1:24-27). This amazing Book is not a science text per se, yet there is nothing in it that contradicts what we know from scientific inquiry.

The theistic worldview has answers for the origin of things from the creation of the universe to the origin of life itself. It explains evil and provides humanity with a moral standard to live by. The theistic worldview of the Christian variety provides believers with a Savior, who's blood is sufficient to wash away their sins. Furthermore, every believer is assured of eternal life (Jn. 3:16).

Contrast that to the worldview of the New Atheists. According to them, life is entirely the result of an inexplicable random coming together of organic molecules. The is no hope for an afterlife. The destiny of mankind is to cease to exist with the eventual death of our sun. There will be no one to remember the deeds of mankind or care.

Hence, the New Atheists offer us nothing but a very old case of hopelessness.

IV. Conspiracies: What Should Be The Christian Response?

Introduction

The growth of the internet has given everyone with a Smartphone the ability to access a library of information. Unfortunately, this technology has also made it possible for conspiracy "theories" to become popular based on inaccurate information or a misinterpretation of facts, through ignorance, malice, or some desire to gain an advantage or an audience. We put this in quotes because *theory* is really not an accurate description of many of the conspiracy narratives being propounded today.

The word *theory* relates to hypothetical circumstances that may or may not be true, or to ideas formed by speculation. As a concept of science, a theory is a set of facts, propositions, or principles analyzed in their relation to one another used to explain phenomena. Under this definition, a theory is something that tends to be confirmed by experimentation (i.e, the assembling of confirming evidence).

Conspiracy connotes a cabal of miscreants plotting to commit some nefarious act by means of stealth and misdirection. Now it is obvious that conspiracies do occur. Criminal gangs are ongoing criminal conspiracies. The Rico Act passed by Congress in 1970 recognizes that cliques of criminal plotters do exist and this Racketeer Influenced and Corrupt Organizations Act was passed to address that.

However, the kind of conspiracies becoming increasingly popular recently, more often than not, seem to a large degree untethered from reality, or having only a rather tenuous relation to it at best. In other words, the evidence for them is based on a good deal of speculation or assumption. In fact, much of this evidence is often cherry picked to reach a foregone conclusion. Lack of evidence for the conspiracy can somehow become evidence, since the "they" or "them" behind it are assumed to be diabolically clever at covering their tracks, or so powerful that they can buy, suppress, or kill to cover it up.

Cherry picking facts to reach a conclusion is an example of the fallacy of *stacking the deck*. This form of reasoning is also called *argument by half-truth, fallacy of exclusion*, or *slanting*.

So, it is obvious we must tread lightly when contemplating whether or not we accept the truth of a conspiracy theory/narrative. After all, the Apostle Paul gives us this admonition: "But refuse foolish and ignorant speculations, knowing that they produce quarrels" (II Tim. 2:23, NASB).

So, with these thoughts in mind, let us evaluate some current conspiracy theories.

The Moon Landing Conspiracy

Christians, along with everyone else who is concerned about truth and advancing knowledge, ought to vigorously denounce those who deny the moon landings that took place between 1969-1972. Their denial undermines the quest for knowledge. A family raising children in such an atmosphere will surely pass on a mountain of misinformation and distrust in science, engineering, and the methods these disciplines employ.

Furthermore, the moon landing deniers erode trust in history. Not a small part of the growth of the popularity of conspiracy theories as a whole has much to do with moon landing denial.

Critical thinking is fundamental to education. However, we don't want to accept everything just because it comes from an authoritative source. Science as a discipline can be subverted as can anything else. After all, it would seem obvious that men and women should not be competing against one another in college and professional sports, especially contact sports. Yet, it seems highly-placed academicians and politicians have no problem with this, and many seem to have a great deal of trouble even defining simple concepts like "male" or "female!" So, Christians must exercise a great deal of discernment in these times. Jesus gave us this bit of sage advice: "Be ye therefore wise as a serpent, and harmless as doves" (Mt. 10:16).

Not long ago a COVID-19 treatment was unveiled based on mRNA research. This treatment has been known to cause serious side effects since it was first introduced experimentally in the 1960s and 70s. So, to have a healthy mistrust of medical treatments based on messenger RNA molecules would seem to be prudent, even if an authority may recommend it. It's not necessary to check your brain at the clinic door.

The response of the CCP masters of China certainly has the earmarks of a conspiratorial mindset when it came to the outbreak of COVID-19 in Wuhan in 2019 and 2020. The authorities there denied it came from a lab, even though Wuhan has an important laboratory known to do research on corona viruses (and known for lax safety protocols as well). These same authorities locked things down in the city and restricted internal travel, while at the same time allowing international air travel to distant foreign cities. This is only explicable if these same authorities wanted to see this virus spread abroad. So, do we see here a conspiracy by government?

So, conspiracies do exist, and misinformation masking as science also exists. However, to deny the achievements of NASA and of brave and dedicated men and women because we acknowledge that is a *non sequitor*.

The Apollo 11 landing was witnessed via television by millions worldwide on July 20, 1969. Hearing Neil Armstrong say, "That's one small step for man, one giant step for mankind," as he stepped from the Lunar Module was unforgettable. For the first time in history, human beings had set foot on an alien world! We were memorized by the footage of the lunar landscape. To see the flag of the United States there on the lunar surface made every red-blooded American chest swell with pride.

To even think the national flag would be a source of doubt about this event back then would have seemed unthinkable!

To be sure, there were critics of the space program back then, claiming the money would be better spent on the needy. However, there could not have been more than one in a million that day who would have doubted the event itself.

So, what evidence do the moon-landing deniers have for this particular conspiracy theory?

The most important piece of "evidence" is the so-called "waving flag" on an airless moon. According to the Apollo 11 deniers, this movement must indicate the moon landing footage was filmed in a studio, some even propose it was directed by the noted film director Stanley Kubrick.

This notion can be easily debunked. There was a horizontal bar extending from along the top of the flag pole which is plainly seen in photos and the film taken of the event. The "waving" movement of the flag was a result of the pole being trust into the lunar regolith. The movement of the flag ceased once the astronauts stopped moving the pole. Very simple explanation. Its called transfer of energy, which works the same on the moon as it does on the earth. That's definitely not proof the event was filmed in a studio at Area 51 or anywhere else.

The second most common "proof" the moon landing was staged is that no stars are seen in the background in any of the photos or footage taken on the lunar surface. The conspiracists claim that since NASA could not figure out how to exactly replicate the star-filled lunar sky, it was decided to just film a black background in the studio and hope no one would notice.

Actually, had this been faked, a star-studded lunar sky added by set designers and decorators would have been a dead giveaway. Rob Webb explains:

> "Anyone who's taken pictures of the stars when the bright moon is out knows that you need to take a very long exposure. In other words, the moon is over exposed, thus causing part of the night sky to get washed out. So, to take photos of a very bright scene, the camera needs a fast shutter speed and very small aperture."

(And, as we have already seen in Section III, the human eye is very much like a camera, only far more sophisticated. This is why few stars are seen in the night sky in the city with the naked eye. Years ago I worked up in Dutch Harbor, Alaska. I was expecting to see the northern lights, but to my disappointment, this well-lit Aleutian harbor (one of the busiest sea-food shipping centers in the world) washed out this spectacle as well as a view of all but the brightest stars).

Everything was brightly lit because it was daytime on the moon. Although the moon's *albedo* is not particularly high (it reflects about 12 percent of the sunlight hitting it), the reflected sunlight is still intense enough to require a long camera exposure in order to capture pictures of the stars. The astronauts were using normal photography settings because they were not concerned at the time with conspiracists using lack of stars as some kind of evidence of fakery.

Another "proof" offered by the lunar-landing deniers is that no astronaut could survive the Van Allen radiation belts that surround the earth. These belts are regions of intense radiation that surround the earth containing charged particles captured by the earth's magnetic field. These areas of strong radiation extend from about 1,000 to about 8,000 miles (the inner belt) and 12,000 to 25,000 miles for the outer belt (*ibid.*).

While prolonged exposure to this radiation would definitely be lethal to any space traveler, the flights to the moon were planned to both avoid going through the outer belt, which is the most dangerous of the two, and to limit the time spent in the less dangerous inner belt. They went through this belt quickly (about 25,000 mph). Furthermore, the spacecraft itself provided a measure of protection against this radiation.

These conspiracists also point out that since we haven't returned to the moon in over fifty years, that this constitutes another piece of evidence that man has never trodden upon the lunar surface. "Why haven't we gone back?" is their constant retort. There are good reasons why further manned Apollo missions were cancelled. For one thing, NASA faced budget cuts. Although in hindsight we might think the Apollo space program was overwhelmingly supported by the people. However, even at the height of its popularity, these missions were actually only supported by a little over half of the population.

We also must realize that manned space travel is a dangerous and potentially deadly undertaking. The Apollo 13 mission came close to having a tragic ending, and we would say only the providence of God averted that tragedy. Unmanned missions have been found to be very effective, costing far less in public treasure, and having the additional benefit of not putting astronaut lives in danger.

Even the Soviet Union cancelled its manned lunar program at this time, believing there was neither glory nor propaganda value in being second place in the race to the moon.

After the cancellation of the Apollo 18 and 19 missions, NASA focused on the Space Shuttle program and later on the ISS (International Space Station).

The moon-landing deniers have many more phony lines of evidence they dredge up, but debunking all of them would be tedious and unnecessary.

What ought the Christian response be to these lunar-landing conspiracists? At least two born-again, Bible-believing Christians stood on the lunar surface and surveyed its marvels with their own eyes. Charlie Duke and Jim Irwin were Apollo astronauts. They have shared their testimonies and have written books about their experiences. The following are Duke's own words:

> "Some people are questioning the fact that we landed on the moon, alleging that it is a big hoax. Well, we did land on the moon six times, and the evidences are overwhelming. If we faked the landing, why did we fake it six times? One needs only to look at the photos from the Lunar Reconnaissance Orbiter from my mission. The photos of our landing site show the descent stage, the lunar rover, the experiments package, and the tracks we

left on the moon. Every landing site has similar evidences" (Faulkner, July 2024).

There were at least 400,000 people who worked on the Apollo program. Many were professing Christians. To believe that all of these thousands of individuals were involved in trying to pull off a scam strains credulity. There is an old adage, that two people can keep a secret only if one of them is dead   More than likely, even the surviving member of that two-person conspiracy would eventually spill the proverbial beans, knowing how people are prone to shoot off their mouths!

The Bible says, "Thou shalt not bear false witness against thy neighbor" (Ex. 20:16). The epitome of being a bearer of false witness is the moon-landing denier. This person impugns the character of honorable people who worked hard to put men on our closest cosmic neighbor. So, professing Christians who engage in this ought to consider that and repent.

The Flat Earth Conspiracy

Flat earthers, or flatties, as I like to call them, are a diverse lot. Many claim to be Christians and offer biblical support for their belief. Others are New Agers or follow other forms of spirituality. Some are atheists. However, since our concern here is with Christian apologetics, those flatties who claim the Bible as their authority will be our main focus here.

A flat earth, or a world supported by a giant turtle swimming an endless sea, or an earth supported by massive elephants, or even other bizarre notions were common in ancient times. However, beginning in the 6th century BC Greek philosophers began to reckon that the world they resided upon was actually spherical. Pythagoras, who was living at this time, surmised a global world. No reasons why he believed this are known, but he likely had some way he calculated this. It is possible he came to that conclusion solely because a sphere was thought to be the perfect shape.

Aristotle (384-322 BC) based his belief in a spherical earth on observation. He noticed that the earth's shadow cast on the moon during eclipses was always round. It never appeared oblong or as a disk. Hence, he concluded the shape of the world must be round. He also observed that a ship disappearing over the horizon hull first indicated a curved earth.

Ptolemy also came to that conclusion early in the 2nd century AD. He noticed that different constellations become visible in the night sky as one travels from north to south, indicating a curved earth. He also noticed some stars were always visible on a clear night (the circumpolar stars), while others are only visible at certain times of the year. He concluded that this allowed a curved earth to face different parts of the night sky during different seasons.

Eratosthenes (c.275-c.195 BC) was the first to accurately measure the circumference of the earth by comparing the angle of the sun's rays at noon on the summer solstice in two separate locations in Egypt. By assuming a spherical earth, and by knowing the distance between Alexandria and Syene (modern-day Aswan) he was able to accomplish this amazing feat. The sun was directly overhead at Syene (being on the Tropic of Cancer) and showed no shadow at the bottom of a well. The shadow at the bottom of a well in Alexandria showed an angle of about 7.2 degrees, or about 1/50 of a circle. By determining that Syene was about 5,000 stadia from Alexandria, he calculated the earth was about 250,000 stadia in circumference. A stadium was between 500 to 600 feet, which would put his calculation between 24,000 to 29,000 miles around. Since we now know the circumference of the earth is actually about 24,900 miles at the equator, Eratosthenes was remarkably close!

Nineteenth century critics of the Bible invented the notion that during the Middle Ages it was commonly believed that the world was a flat plane. Washington Irving popularized this idea in his fictionalized biography of Christopher Columbus. Irving used this biography to set up a fake conflict between a globe-believing Columbus and a flat-earth believing clergy, and that he would prove them wrong by sailing around the earth. Of course, Columbus had no intension of sailing around the world; he was looking for a shortcut to the Indies with its riches in spices and gold.

John Draper took up Irving's mantle and wrote *History of the Conflict Between Religion and Science* in 1874. Draper's one-sided "history" was filled with misinformation designed to put Christianity and the Bible in the worst possible light.

However, the Dark Ages were not so dark that people believed in a flat earth. It was commonly understood then that the world was a sphere. The knowledge of the Greeks and Romans had been passed down by monks and other clerics. They were mistaken about the *geocentricity* of the universe, but they had the shape of the earth and its dimensions down pretty well. If fact, the scholars of the church opposed Columbus only regarding his mistaken belief that the earth was about 6,000 leagues (about 18,000 miles) in circumference. They were concerned he would become lost in a vast western ocean full of unknown perils. Columbus knew of northern barren lands in this ocean from his journey to Iceland earlier in his nautical career, and he wanted to avoid these places. However, no one at the time knew of two vast continents that would bar the way of Columbus from reaching the lands of silks, gemstones, precious metals, and aromatic spices.

A man by the name of Samuel Rowbotham (1816-1884) took it upon himself to prove the earth was flat. He was already a convinced flatty himself. Rowbotham watched a small boat sail the entire six-mile distance of the Old Bedford River. Since this small boat should have disappeared below the horizon, he claimed he had proven the world to be flat!

Rowbotham committed a major scientific faux pas--he did not repeat the experiment in order to account for variables.

However, after adjusting for the phenomenon of atmospheric refraction (the variable), Alfred R. Wallace calculated the correct curvature expected of a spherical earth in 1870.

Rowbotham wrote *Zetetic Astronomy Earth Not a Globe* under the pseudonym Paralax.in 1865. His view of the world was a flat disc centered at the north pole bounded around its perimeter by the supposed Antarctic Ice Wall. The moon, sun, planets, and stars were a few thousand miles above the surface of this earth-disk.

Rowbotham's life was filled with scandal. In 1861 he married a 15-year old girl with whom he had been living prior to the marriage. She bore him at least 15 children, of whom only four survived. He was named in a number of wrongful death cases, including the accidental poisoning of his own child. He also peddled quack cures for diseases and invented dubious medical devices.

He did found the Universal Zetetic Society that continued under Lady Elizabeth Blout after his death. After World War I the Society declined in membership, but revived in 1956 under the name The Flat Earth Society. Rowbotham is considered the modern founder of the flat earth movement.

Eric Dubay is responsible for the most recent iteration of the flat-earth movement. This man is a yoga instructor who resides in Thailand. After reading Rowbotham's book, he became convinced of his flat earth cosmology. Dubay is more New Ager than Christian, but his biblical arguments for a flat earth have tickled the ears of some Christians. Since things both true and false have equal access on YouTube, this man's well-made videos have been well received by many willing to be deceived.

So, you'd think that pictures taken of the earth from space would convince anyone of the true shape of our world. However, flatties are not swayed by this. Why? Because they are convinced NASA is some kind of nefarious organization run by Masons. (And there is no group more beset with conspiracy theories than the flat-earth movement). Yet, the first photo showing the curvature of earth was taken by U.S. Army Captain Albert Stevens on Dec. 30, 1931 while flying at about 23,000 feet over Argentina. This was almost three decades before the founding of NASA.

The First photo taken from a rocket which showed the curvature of the earth was taken by a camera from a captured V-2 rocket on Oct. 24, 1946. The V-2 was launched from White Sands Missile Range, New Mexico and reached an altitude of 65 miles. This is just above the *Karmen Line,* which is 100 kilometers (62 miles) above sea level, the boundary between space and the earth's atmosphere. This was also well before the founding of NASA in 1958.

Also, if flatties were really serious about proving the earth is a large dirt pizza, all they would have to do is produce one high-altitude aerial photograph showing a flat world. None exists and none will be forthcoming because the world is spherical and even many flatties probably know that already in their heart of hearts.

But, Christian flatties are not convinced by any scientific or photographic evidence because they believe scripture backs their claim.

For example, Revelation 7:1 and 20:7& 8 describe "the four corners of the earth." Since the Bible mentions four corners, then the earth cannot be a sphere. However, what are Christian flatties saying here? Is the earth like a big pizza, or is it a square like a checkerboard? The Greek word *gonia* means primarily a "corner," like the corner of a house, or the angle of a rectangle. However, in this context, the word signifies "the extreme limits of the earth" (Vine, pg. 233).

The Bible uses the expression "the ends of the earth" many times. Christian flatties reckon a round earth would have no ends, but a flat one surely would.

This phrase is not meant to be taken as a literal physical location, but is used to represent the furthest and most distant parts of the world (see Ps. 2:8; Job 28:24; Acts 1:8). The original authors meant these passages to represent *geographical distance* and not a place where the earth ends, and church expositors have always concurred with this interpretation.

We read in the book of Genesis: "And God said, Let there be a firmament in the midst of the waters, and let it divide the waters from the waters" (1:6). Most flat earth advocates see "firmament" (Heb. *raqia*) as a solid dome over the flat plane of the earth. In fact, their whole notion of the dome comes from this word. However, the Hebrew *raqia* actually denotes "that which is spread out," therefore, most newer Bible translations translate this word as "expanse."

In the following verses God places the sun, moon, and other heavenly bodies in the *raqia* and has birds flying across it. It is obvious the *raqia* is both what we would call outer space and the atmosphere. There is nothing in the text that would indicate Moses was describing a dome over the flat plane of the world (Faulkner, Nov. 1, 2018).

A truly ridiculous flat-earth Bible proof is the World Tree that Nebuchadnezzar saw in his dream (Dan. 4:1-27). The Babylonian king said this, "The tree grew, and was strong, and the height thereof reached unto heaven, and the sight thereof to the end of all the earth" (vs. 11). Flat earth logic here insists that it would be impossible for the whole world to see this tree if the earth were a globe, but quite possible on a flat one!

Unfortunately, a tree appearing in a dream can hardly be evidence for the actual shape of the physical earth. This is not an actual tree as Daniel's dream interpretation indicates (vss. 20-22). The tree is interpreted as King Nebuchadnezzar himself. Besides this, even on a flat earth there could be no tree high enough to be visible to all of its inhabitants. *Perspective*, a term flatties are fond of tossing around loosely, would prohibit this.

Christian flatties also use Psalm 104:5 to assert the earth is not a "spinning wet ball": "He set the earth on foundations, that it cannot be moved forever." However, a lexical examination of *timmot* shows that it can mean "to waver, to slip, shake, fall." The basic root *mot* can have a variety of meanings: Lev 25:35: "If thy brother be waxen poor, and *fallen in decay* with thee; then thou shalt relieve him."; Deut. 32:35: "Their foot *shall slide* in due time."; Job 41:23: God says this to Job concerning leviathan, "The flakes of his flesh are joined together: they are firm in themselves; they cannot *be moved*" (i.e., "removed"); Ps. 17:5: "Hold up my goings in thy paths, that my footsteps *slip* not."; Ps. 46:5: "God is in the midst of her; she shall not *be moved*." This word is also translated *tottered, out of course, gives way*, and *staggering*. It is evident the Hebrew word *mot* has the meaning of "to move (or walk) unsteadily, to wobble, to be unstable so as to be about to fall." So, according to *Barnes' Notes on the Bible*:

"So that it cannot be shaken out of its place. That is, it is fixed, permanent, solid. Its foundations do not give way, as edifices reared by man, but it abides the same age to age-the most fixed and stable object of which we have knowledge."

So, it is evident the word *timmot* here sees the world as *enduring* and *not staggering so as to fall*; i.e, it will remain forever until a new heaven and earth is established at the end of days (Rev. 21:1). This is not a proof text against the established facts of the earth's 24-hour rotation on its axis, nor of its 365¼ day revolution around the sun. Furthermore, this verse actually says nothing about whether the earth is globe or flat.

The temptation of Jesus in the Judean wilderness is another proof text of the Christian flatty: "The devil taketh him up into an exceeding high mountain, and sheweth him all the kingdoms of the world, and the glory of them" (Mt. 4:8). Again, according to flat-earth believers, it would not be possible for the devil to show Jesus all the world's kingdoms on a globe earth, but it *would* be possible on a flat plane. Of course, even on a flat earth, it would not be possible to see every kingdom, even atop Mt. Everest. Since even flatties recognize day and night on their dirt pizza, at least half the earth would be hidden by darkness. So, it is evident the devil did not actually show the Lord every kingdom on the earth, but that the prince of darkness was using some kind of sleight of hand to conjure up an image of the world's powers and principalities.

It is evident the Bible says nothing, whether explicitly or implicitly, about the earth being flat like a pancake. Furthermore, there *is* some evidence the Bible recognizes a spherical earth: "It is he [God] who sitteth upon the circle of the earth" (Isa. 40:22). The Hebrew word *chug* has the following meanings: "vault, sphere," or "arch."

According to Gil's *Exposition of the Entire Bible*: "It is he that sitteth upon the circle of the earth,…. Or, "the globe" of it; for the earth is spherical or globular, not a flat plain, but round, hung as a ball in the air."

Leading Hebraist Xanthe Pagnino (1470-1536) translates *chug* here with the Latin *sphaera*, which means "sphere, globe, ball, orb, celestial globe, orbit." Church Father Montanus Vatablus uses the word *globus*, meaning "sphere" or "globe." Campegius Vitringa (1659-1722), Dutch Hebraist and theologian, translates *chug ha'arets* by the Latin *orbem telluris* ("globe of the earth").

The idea of a round or spherical earth is also reflected in the *Douay-Rheims Bible*: "It is he that sitteth upon the globe of the earth." *Peshitta Holy Bible Translated*: "And him who sits on the sphere of the Earth."

The majority of translations use "circle" with a few opting for "vault." However, the point of the passage is not the *shape* of the earth, but the fact that God rules *over* the earth. For example: "He sits enthroned above the circle of the earth" (*Berean Study Bible*) or *GOD'S WORD Translation*: "God is enthroned above the earth, and those who live on it are like grasshoppers." So, this verse is contrasting the greatness of God with the smallness of those who dwell upon His world.

Many flat-earthers also deny fundamentals like the force of gravity. It is evident why they would hold to such an odd notion. Their characterization of the impossibility of the earth being "a spinning wet ball" depends upon a denial of this *fundamental force* of the universe.

However, the force of gravity can be measured with a gravimeter. A gravimeter is a scientific instrument used to measure variations in the earth's gravitational field. It detects small changes in the strength of gravity at various locations. Gravimeters use pendulums, electronics, or springs to measure gravitational attraction.

Everything that has *mass* has gravity. The greater the mass of an object, the stronger will be the pull of its gravitational force. The more mass an object has, the more the force of gravity it will exert on objects around it.

Gravity is measured by calculating the acceleration it exerts on a freely falling object, formerly measured by 32 feet per second per second, but now at 9.8 meters per second squared (9.8 m/s^2). This can vary slightly due to differences in mass distribution on the earth.

Gravity effects time, and this can be measured by sophisticated clocks. Since where gravity is stronger, time runs slower. On the surface of the earth time runs more slowly than it does at altitude. This was postulated by Albert Einstein with his General Theory of Relativity in 1905. Although Einstein stated that gravity is not a force, but rather a curvature of spacetime caused by mass and energy, for all practical purposes, gravity is a force.

Sophisticated atomic clocks can measure the difference in time between the earth's surface and higher altitudes. By comparing the tick rate of two such identical clocks, one placed at a higher altitude and another placed at a lower altitude, it has been discovered that higher gravity slows down time. In other words, time moves more quickly at higher altitudes. Of course, not at a rate anyone would notice. We are only talking about a second or two in a million.

This definitely proves that the force of gravity exists. Since gravity tends to pull things toward the center of mass, that is another indication the earth is a sphere, conforming to what we observe with other large celestial bodies in the solar system and the rest of the universe.

Miscellaneous Conspiracy Theories

The Chemtrail Conspiracy Theory

The chemtrail conspiracy theory became popularized after the U.S. Air Force published a report in 1996 regarding weather modification (Smith, Sep. 24, 2013). This led to a rumor circulating in the late 1990s accusing the USAF of spraying mysterious chemical substances which made unusual contrail patterns (Simons, Sep. 27, 2013). This was conflated by conspiracists into a government program of spraying birth-control substances or drugs of various types to produce a passive populace. These substances are said by conspiracy theorists to cause physical and psychological problems to the population (Schlatter, Mar. 9, 2001).

These theories began to be posted soon after this in chat rooms, message boards and other public internet forums and were promoted by Richard Finke and William Thomas. Late-night radio host Art Bell, who never met a conspiracy theory he didn't run with, popularized the chemtrail conspiracy theory beginning around 1999.

In fact, the very term "chemtrail" was first accidentally coined by Bell on his *Coast to Coast* radio show sometime just before the year 2000. He got a call from a man who mentioned *contrails*. Mishearing the caller, Bell said, "Chemtrails?" The caller, evidently not hearing Bell properly, affirmed this. After this, Bell recognized the value his new accidental term had for his show about government cover-ups and conspiracies. Caller after caller began to phone Bell with their own stories about "chemtrails" (Freerepublic.com, 1/14/2025).

However, the "chemtrail" conspiracy theory may have an element of truth to it.

According to a Forbes article (Jan. 11, 2021) multibillionaire Bill Gates is putting a large amount of money behind "the development of sun-dimming technology that would potentially reflect sunlight out of Earth's atmosphere, triggering a global cooling effect." This program, called The Stratospheric Controlled Perturbation Experiment, is being run by Harvard University researchers. By spraying calcium carbonate ($CaCO_3$) dust into the atmosphere, it is hoped a sun-reflecting effect may mitigate global warming.

There are proponents and antagonists to this program. The antagonists claim that atmospheric polluters will have no incentive to stop, since they could offset the dirty air their activities produce with the magic of sun-reflecting dust. The proponents point to the actual global cooling effects of volcanic eruptions that put particulates into the atmosphere on a scale that actually lowered global average temperatures. However, the eruption of Mt. Tambora in the Dutch East Indies in 1815 caused "the year without summer." There were widespread crop failures and near-famines that year (Cohen, Jan. 11, 2021).

This program has not been adopted on any large scale due to the aforementioned risks. But the buzz in cyberspace would make it sound as though we were being drenched in toxic substances designed to sterilize the populace or turn us into zombies. All it takes is any unusual contrail activity in the atmosphere to confirm this "chemtrail" conspiracy, when the whole notion began with Art Bell's misunderstanding of a caller. His accidental invention of a new term reinforced his audience's healthy appetite for the chemtrail and a multitude of other conspiracy theories.

The JFK Assassination Conspiracy Theory

The assassination of John F. Kennedy (JFK) on Nov. 22, 1963 has given rise to many conspiracy theories. So, the best we can do here is just give as brief an overview as possible. The following are alleged to have been involved in the Kennedy assassination: rouge elements of the CIA, the Mafia, Fidel Castro, Vice President Lyndon Johnson, the Soviet KGB, to name just a few. Vincent Bugilosi, the man who prosecuted the Manson Family, has chronicled 42 groups, 82 assassins, and about 214 individuals who have been accused or who have been somehow tied to the supposed JFK plot at one time or another.

Our contention here is that Lee Harvey Oswald was the soul assassin based on the non-speculative evidence available and a time-honored principle of logic--*Occam's Razor*.

The JFK assassination is probably the grandfather of all conspiracy theories, and is probably the main stream from which the vast majority of modern conspiracy theories have been spawned.

The Warren Commission, was authorized to investigate the assassination according to Senate Resolution 137. They presented an 888-page final report on Sep. 24, 1964. The report concluded that Oswald acted alone in assassinating the president. The Commission Report also concluded Jack Ruby acted alone in killing Oswald two days later. It found no evidence of conspiracy involving Oswald or Ruby or that either was any part of a conspiracy, either foreign or domestic, to assassinate JFK.

The following is a brief summary of the Warren Commission's findings (*National Archives*, Sep. 24, 1964):

1) The shots which killed President Kennedy and wounded Texas Governor Connally were fired from the sixth floor of the Texas School Book Depository, the place where Oswald worked.

2) The first bullet that struck Kennedy hit the back of the neck and exited the front of the neck and may not have been fatal. The second bullet entered the right rear of the head and would have been fatal.

3) The bullet that struck Connally entered the right side of his back and traveled downward, exited his right nipple, passed through his right wrist, and entered his left thigh.

4) No credible evidence exists of shots fired from the Triple Underpass ahead of the motorcade or from anywhere else.

5) There is no credible evidence to indicate that more than three shots were fired.

6) There is persuasive evidence that the bullet which struck Connally had pierced the President's throat. Although the Texas governor's testimony had given rise to some difference of opinion on the matter, there is no question by any of the members of the Commission that every shot that wounded both the President and the Governor that day were fired from the sixth floor of the Texas School Book Depository.

7) Oswald fired the shots that killed Kennedy and wounded Connally. .

8) Oswald murdered Dallas PD Patrolman J. D. Tippet about 45 minutes after the assassination

9) Jack Ruby, a night club owner, entered the basement of the Dallas PD and shot Oswald.

10) There is no previous connection to either Oswald or Ruby, or that either was a part of a conspiracy to assassinate the president.

11) There was no evidence found of subversion or conspiracy on the part of any Federal, state, local agency, or official.

12) Oswald's motives could not be determined, although he lived in the Soviet Union and was known to sympathize with the Communist regime of Fidel Castro of Cuba.

Oswald had a troubled upbringing. He was a habitual truant until he quit school altogether and joined the Marine Corps in 1956 at age 17. He received two court-martials and did time in the brig twice. While in the service, he received the nickname *Oswaldskovich* because of his pro-Soviet sympathies. After his release from active duty, Oswald defected to the USSR in 1959. He claimed to Soviet authorities that he was a Communist (he considered himself a socialist by age 15). There he married a Russian woman. In 1962 he returned to the United States with his wife and child..

Oswald made an attempt to assassinate retired Maj. General Edwin Walker on Apr. 10, 1963 with the same rifle he used to assassinate Kennedy. Walker was only slightly wounded. Oswald's wife testified her husband had traveled to Walker's house and took a shot at him.

Walker's assassination attempt was not solved until after Oswald's arrest. The bullet was too damaged to do a striation analysis, but neutron activation analysis showed it was "extremely likely" that it was made by the same manufacturer and was the same caliber of the two bullets that struck Kennedy (Guinn, Sep. 29, 2007).

Although conspiracy theories regarding the Kennedy assassination began to circulate almost immediately after the event, New Orleans District Attorney Jim Garrison is a prominent person responsible for popularizing the idea of a wider plot behind the president's death.

Garrison zealously pursued an assassination conspiracy theory that involved the Central Intelligence Agency (CIA). To that end, he prosecuted New Orleans businessman Clay Shaw in 1969. Shaw was acquitted less than an hour after the case was given to the jury (*Penthouse*, November 1969).

The chief witness against Shaw was Perry Russo, who testified that he attended a party at the apartment of an anti-Castro activist by the name of David Ferrie. It was at this party that Oswald (introduced as Leon Oswald), Ferrie, and a Mr. Clem Bertrand (identified as Shaw by Russo) discussed plans for assassinating President Kennedy (*Louisiana vs. Clay L. Shaw*).

However, Russo's testimony had been tainted by hypnosis and by use of the drug sodium pentothal, sometimes inaccurately called the "truth serum." An earlier version of Russo's testimony failed to mention this party at David Ferrie's apartment (where the alleged assassination plot unfolded).

Garrison defended this conduct, stating:

> "Before we introduced the testimony of our witnesses, we made them undergo independent verifying tests, including polygraph examination, truth serum, and

hypnosis. We thought this would be hailed as an unprecedented step in jurisprudence; instead, the press turned around and hinted that we had drugged our witnesses or given them posthypnotic suggestions to testify falsely" (Norden, October 1967).

Any witness subjected to such a regimen could only be described as unreliable.

In January of 1968 Garrison subpoenaed Kerry Thornley, who knew Oswald from their time in the USMC. Garrison wanted him to appear before a grand jury to question him about what he knew about Oswald and others who may have been involved in the assassination plot (*The Miami News*, Jan. 10, 1968). Garrison charged Thornley with perjury after he denied being in contact with Oswald since 1959. The perjury charge was eventually dropped by Garrison's successor.

Clay Shaw and Kerry Thornley were the only persons ever charged (aside from Oswald himself) in connection with the Kennedy assassination, and both of those cases fell apart.

It is evident that there is no solid evidence to accuse anyone of being party to the assassination of President John F. Kennedy other than Lee Harvey Oswald. Anyone, but especially the Christian, who accuses any person, whether living or dead, of being part of such a conspiracy is bearing false witness, according to Ex. 20:16. The Law specified that the punishment of a false witness is to be carried out without pity: "Your eye shall not pity. It shall be life for life, eye for eye, tooth for tooth, hand for hand, foot for foot" (Deut. 19:21).

The Protocols of the Elders of Zion Conspiracy

The Protocols of the Elders of Zion was a text fabricated for the purpose of accusing Jews of plotting global domination. It is a work drawn largely from plagiarizing a number earlier sources. It was first published in Czarist Russia in 1903 and has been translated into many languages. The *Protocols* have played a key role in widely disseminating the belief in a secret international Jewish conspiracy to dominate the world both economically and politically.

Though this work of fiction was written over a century ago, and would seem to be "ancient history," yet, it continues to motivate anti-Semites to this day:

> "The great importance of *The Protocols* lies in its permitting antisemites to reach beyond their traditional circles and find a large international audience, a process that continues to this day. The forgery poisoned public life wherever it appeared; it was "self-generating"; a blueprint that migrated from one conspiracy to another (Eco, pg. 490).

In light of this, the accusations of the *Protocols* reverberate to this day and make this *a contemporary Christian issue.*

The *Protocols* is presented as a factual document supported by evidence, even though it is undeniably fraudulent. This document purportedly was written before 1901, and alludes to the assassinations of King Umberto I of Italy in 1900, and President William McKinley in 1901 as if these two events had been planned out far in advance.

Sergei Aleksandrovich Nilus (1862-1929) was a Russian mystic and anti-Semitic author. His book *The Great within the Small and Anti*christ, an Imminent Possibility. Notes of an Orthodox Believer (1903) is now known for its 1905 edition in which the *Protocols* are included as the last chapter.

Anti-Semitism has always been alive and well in the world, but the idea of a world-wide conspiracy of "international Jewry" plotting to take over every bank and government only had its genesis in the latter third of the 19th century.

Catholics, Protestants, and especially Jews were viewed with suspicion in Czarist Russia. They were seen as not quite loyal to the Russian Empire; a potential source of foreign subversion. Jews who followed their traditional religion were seen as an even more alien element.

Jacob Baufman, a Lithuanian Jew from Minsk, had a dispute with his local Jewish council (called a *qahal*). Consequently, he converted to Russian Orthodoxy and began to attack Judaism in print. He wrote two books in 1868-69 that claimed unscrupulous Jewish leaders were out to grab the property of honest Orthodox Christian businessmen with the ultimate aim of seizing political control. He further claimed that this was part of an international conspiratorial organization based in Paris called the *Israelite Universal Alliance* under prominent Jewish Freemason Adolphe Cremieux.

Baufman's works were translated into English, French, German, and other languages, giving rise to the idea of an international Jewish shadow government. The ideas propagated by his books began to be taken seriously by Russian officials. About this time (March 1881) a *nihilist* terror organization (*Nardonaya Volya*, "The People's Will") used a bomb to assassinate Czar Alexander II. Soon, Jews were tied to the plot. *Pogroms* began thereafter, and many Jewish villages and towns were attacked and burned.

As Russian fortunes declined in the late 19th and early 20th centuries, Jews were a handy scapegoat to blame for the situation the nation found itself in. The publication of the *Protocols* in serial form by the newspaper *Znarnya* in 1903 fueled this attitude. Russia's defeat in the Russo-Japanese War and the subsequent Revolution of 1905 confirmed in the minds of many Russians that the plot outlined in the *Protocols* was reality.

After the defeat of the monarchist White Russian forces in 1920 by the Bolsheviks, the *Protocols* began to be disseminated in the West by those escaping the new regime. Since many of the Bolsheviks had been raised as Jews, it was concluded by many new-found non-Russian readers, that the Revolution was part of some insidious larger plan.

Even automobile manufacturer Henry Ford became convinced in the truth of the *Protocols*. He published a series of anti-Semitic articles in the *Dearborn Independent* beginning in 1920, drawing heavily on quotes and citations from the *Protocols*. He later repudiated the articles in 1927 after bowing to public pressure (Singerman, *American Jewish History*).

The sources for the *Protocols* are the following: 160 passages from *Dialogue in Hell Between Machiavelli and Montesquieu* by French author Maurice Joly (1864), and a chapter from *Biarritz* by anti-Semitic German author Herrmann Goedsche (1868).

The *Protocols* began to be exposed early on as a hoax. When Nilus published the complete text in 1905, he claimed it was a work of the First Zionist Congress held in Basel, Switzerland in 1897. However, this is not possible, since the First Zionist Congress was a well attended public event with many non-Jews as part of the gathering. Nilus then claimed the *Protocols* were the work of later Zionist Congresses in 1902-03, contradicting his earlier claim of receiving a copy in 1901.

In 1921 a series of articles in the British newspaper *The Times* exposed the *Protocols* as a plagiarism from Joly's *Dialogue in Hell*. The German newspaper *Frankfurter Zeitung* came to the same conclusion in 1924.

A trial in Berne, Switzerland beginning Oct. 29, 1934, also exposed the fraud that is the *Protocols*. A Swiss political party (The National Front) was charged with selling copies during a political meeting, violating a law of the city. Two Jewish organizations were plaintiffs. Two defendants were convicted of violating a Bernese statute that prohibited passing out "immoral, obscene, or brutalizing" literature on May 19, 1935 (Hafner, Dec. 28, 2005). Three other defendants were acquitted.

The Swiss court concluded the *Protocols* were a plagiarized forgery and obscene literature. The presiding judge saw through this literary monstrosity, and though recognizing the damage the *Protocols* had done (and would continue to do), nonetheless, called them "nothing but laughable nonsense" (Kadzhaya, Dec. 17, 2005).

Russian exile Vladimir Burtsev, who hated both Bolshevism and Fascism, was a witness for the plaintiffs in the Berne case. His testimony became the basis of a book *The Protocols of the Elders of Zion: A Proved Forgery* published in Paris in 1938.

Adolph Hitler was so convinced of the truth of the *Protocols* that He mentioned them in *Mein Kampf* (Vol. I, pgs. 307-08). This forgery was an important thread of evidence to his worldview. Although he rarely mentioned the *Protocols* in his speeches, nevertheless, he was convinced of a conspiracy by "international Jewry" to bring Germany down. He was so convinced of this, that he and other Nazi leaders concocted the "Final Solution" of eliminating all the Jews of Europe in death camps. Since he was also convinced that Communism was also part of the wider Jewish conspiracy, Operation Barbarossa, the invasion of the Soviet Union in June of 1941, was a necessity according to Hitler's fevered conspiratorial mind.

The *Protocols* conspiracy has given rise to many modern conspiracy theories related to a so-called Jewish-Masonic controlled New World Order. This Jewish-Masonic conspiracy asserts that Freemasons are a front for the international Jewish conspiracy (Poli, 2014).

Holocaust denial is a natural outcome of the "conspiracy" outlined in the *Protocols*. The holocaust deniers make one or more of the following claims: (1) the Nazi program of eliminating the Jews was only one of deportation from Germany, and not a mass killing, (2) the Jews died of typhus and other diseases in the camps, not by the use of gas chambers and other means of execution, (3) the number Jews executed is far less than the official figure of six million, and (4) the Holocaust is the biggest hoax ever perpetrated, and it was done to make the world feel guilty in order to create the State of Israel as a sop to assuage this collective guilt.

It is evident that Christians ought to reject *The Protocols of the Elders of Zion* because it is a hoax perpetrated by Jew-haters to justify their hatred. It is based on *hidden knowledge known only by the enlightened few.*

This sounds a lot like the heresy of *Gnosticism* with a new twist. Gnosticism was an ancient cult and rival to Christianity. The *soteriology* of this cult was by attainment of esoteric knowledge that would free the soul trapped by the material world. For the Jew-hater, the trap is set by the mercantile Jew with his emporium of material goods. Freedom, or escape from this materialist trap, is a rejection of the mercantilist Jew with his capitalism and all of the works it finances, such as war, Bolshevism, the New World Order, material excess, pornography, the sexual revolution, etc.

Devotees of *The Protocols of the Elders of Zion* see in this conspiracy a kind of *Rosetta stone* of modern history. Just as the Rosetta stone unlocked the secrets of deciphering Egyptian hieroglyphics, the *Protocols* unlock the mysteries of both present and past history for the true believer.

However, the *Protocols* have been a justification for the persecution of Jews, even though there is hardly a word of truth to be found in them.

Christians should never allow themselves to be caught up in conspiracies involving a so-called plot of international wealthy and influential Jews. That goes for Holocaust denial as well. Both of these ideas can be traced back to the forgery that is the *Protocols*. Instead of using over a century of lies to justify a prejudice, we should consider what God said to Balaam concerning His people Israel: "Thou shalt not go with them; thou shalt not curse the people: for they are blessed" (Numbers 22:12).

Conclusion

There is no question that people love conspiracy theories. They seem to make sense of a world that is often senseless. However, there is precious little evidence to commend these conspiracies. The moon landing conspiracy would have had to involve hundreds of thousands of people with nary a one divulging the secret to the press.

Conspiracies can occupy the time and energy of people who could best use these precious commodities doing other things. The great Apostle Paul gives us this advice: "But shun profane and vain babblings; for they will increase unto more ungodliness" (II Tim. 2:16).

Similarly, the Apostle to the Gentiles also says this, "Let no corrupt communication proceed out of your mouth, but that which is good to the use of edifying, that it may minister grace to the hearer" (Eph. 4:26). It is difficult to keep our speech completely free of all foolishness, and surely the Lord does not expect that of us. However, to hold to ideas that demonize some, bring false accusations to others, turn honorable men into scoundrels, and presents history as a dark cabal of money-grubbing war mongers stealthily manipulating events has nothing to commend it to the Christian or anyone else who seeks to live according to the dictates of truth.

V. Aliens And UFOs: Are ETs and Little Green Men (LGM) Biblical or Logical?

Introduction

Space aliens are creatures of science fiction, not of science fact. Reports of "alien abductions" are based on nothing more than psychological factors such as nightmares, or particularly disturbing phenomena called "night terrors." Night terrors are nightmares occurring while the subject is partially awake. A person can have a feeling of helplessness while in this state, often accompanied further by sensations of being levitated. Fertile imaginations can fill in the rest of an "alien abduction" narrative.

The science fiction genre has more to do with the current obsession with aliens from outer space than anything from science fact. French novelist Jules Verne (1828-1905), considered the father of this genre, was definitely a theist. However, the next generation of Sci-Fi writers were committed Darwinists and many were militant Communist atheists.

This is reflected in H. G. Wells' novel *The Time Machine* (1895), which describes the author's views (in a fictional format) regarding the evolution of the human race into two distinct species some 800,000 years into the future. His next novel, *The War of the Worlds* (1898), is one of the first such works of fiction to depict the invasion of the earth by aliens from another world. (His novel *The Days of the Comet* (1906) describes a world transformed by the passing of a comet into a place of peace, in line with the Fourth Epoch envisioned by the founder of modern Communism, Karl Marx).

After the Second World War, Hollywood churned out scores of campy science fiction films featuring aliens from outer space, and the public was hooked. The vast majority of UFO sightings, accounts of alien abductions, and alien visitation narratives have been recorded from these and following years.

However, there were late 19th and early twentieth century reports of cigar-shaped UFOs or craft like dirigibles appearing in various places. For example, The Great Airship Mystery was a phenomenon allegedly seen by thousands of people in late 1896 through the middle of 1897. Nighttime sightings of lights in the sky were common. Other accounts described airships or dirigibles crewed by foreign-looking people, some claiming to be Martians.

Although there was some experimentation with dirigibles at the time, such craft were so rare that it was not possible that these few experimental craft could create such a raft of widespread sightings. The most likely explanation of the mystery airships is plain old *yellow journalism.* Newspapers at the time were prone to print sensational stories that stretched the truth, or to run with outright hoaxes to increase circulation and sales. These stories, often accompanied by imaginative illustrations, were not actually meant to be taken seriously Newspapers at the time were often little more than tabloids.

However, these often fabricated mystery airship stories were rediscovered after the Second World War. This provided more proof for UFO devotees that visitations of extraterrestrials had been ongoing and real. Note the mystery airship phenomenon followed what was known to be the advanced technology of the time--airships.

There is no doubt a correlation between the mystery airships, the appetite for science fiction and its extraterrestrial denizens, and the post World War II growth of the aerospace industry. This was a kind of psychological perfect storm. It would seem reports of strange lights in the sky can fuel the imagination of anyone already susceptible to believing in little green men!

Before buying into the idea that we are being monitored by beings from "out there," one ought to first do a little exercise. Ask yourself this: Do the unidentified objects we see in the atmosphere have a natural explanation, or are at least some of them actually piloted by intelligent beings from outer space? We ought to give zero credence to the latter, for the following reasons:

1. Of the some 5,000 *exoplanets* discovered, none of them are fit for life to have developed on them.

2. According to Cambridge professor of astronomy Sir Fred Hoyle, the likelihood of life arising from inanimate matter is on the order of one chance in 10 raised to the power of 40,000! Probabilities this remote have virtually no chance of occurring.

For life to have developed by chance a second time in the universe would even be more unlikely. That life would arise a second time on another planet, such that we would now be visited by intelligent beings from there could be analyzed on the basis of the theory of probability, with the calculation of Hoyle's in mind.

One chance event in a series is called an *iteration*. For example, the iteration of a single coin toss landing on heads is always 1 in 2 even in a two-toss series. However, the second coin toss in the series, which is called a *permutation*, would now have a probability of landing on heads at 1 in 4, because the chance of this particular permutation occurring would be ½ x ½ = ¼.

So the possibility of life arising by chance on the earth is one in 10 to the 40,000th power, so according to probability theory, the possibility of a second such occurrence would be that times itself. To say it simply, the possibility of life occurring a second time in the universe by chance would be a virtual impossibility times a virtual impossibility! And we are not even considering here whether or not this life is intelligent.

For intelligent life to have occurred by chance on this planet is even a more remote possibility than Hoyle's calculation would indicate, because he was only determining the possibility of the simplest single-celled life forming by random chance alone.

Since time is always a factor in probability, it would be just as likely an extraterrestrial civilization would be less advanced than ours and had not yet developed space travel. This is on top of an already infinitesimally-remote chance that such a civilization exists in the first place.

3. The whole concept of space aliens has its basis in the Theory of Evolution, which is based largely on materialist philosophy, and not on the best possible evidence.

4. The SETI (Search for Extra Terrestrial Intelligence) Project has yet to monitor a single intelligently-generated radio signal from outer space in the many years it has been in operation.

Isn't it possible that God could have created other worlds with intelligent life?

Of course that is possible, but this would raise all kinds of theological problems. Would they be fallen beings in need of salvation? Would Christ have died for them as He had the sons of Adam? Would they have eternal souls?

Since the exoplanets so far discovered appear unsuitable for life, and none of the planets of the Solar System, except for earth, are suitable for life, it is a safe bet to conclude our planet is unique in the universe. If God has seen fit to create another world on the other side of the universe with intelligent beings, they would be so far away that there would be no possible chance of coming into contact with them anyway. Hence, it is a matter that is essentially fruitless to consider, though the concept of extraterrestrial life makes interesting speculation and makes for entertaining science fiction.

The Bible mentions the translation of Enoch (Gen. 5:24), and that Elijah was carried off by a "chariot of fire" (II Ki. 2:11). Couldn't these references be referring to alien abductions couched in terms the ancient Bible writers would understand?

Since we have already determined that the possibility of extraterrestrial life existing is for all intent and purposes statistically zero (0), we ought to take the Bible's word on these matters at face value. God took Enoch and Elijah because they exemplified unparalleled righteousness. It is as simple as that. One's entire Christian worldview must be called into question if space aliens are added to it.

Isn't it possible that Ezekiel's vision (ch. 1, vss. 4-28) was actually his sighting of an alien spacecraft?

Some UFO devotees have read this passage and declared it to be a likely sighting by the Hebrew prophet of an alien space craft. Ezekial saw "a whirlwind came out of the north, a great cloud, and a fire unfolding itself" (vs. 4). The unusual way the four living creatures move in the passage seem otherworldly, as indeed it is, just not in the way our alien-hunting friends may think. They cite the description of the "wheels" (vs. 16) as evidence, since both wheels and saucers are round. The "eyes" are described as the windows of this craft.

What Ezekial saw in his vision was a revelation of the shekinah glory of God, just as had Moses (Ex. 3:1-10). Isaiah (Isa. 6:1-10), Daniel (Dan. 10:5-14), and the Apostle John (Rev. 1:12-19). He gives his unique perspective on the matter, but in no way is it different than others who have been privileged to have witnessed this experience. What he saw was certainly not an ancient visitation by extraterrestrial beings.

Conclusion

So, the idea of space aliens has precious little evidence to back it up. In fact, a good deal of hoax and flimflam is attached to this phenomenon. At one time our own Solar System held out the promise of possible advanced civilizations of intelligent alien beings. Venus and Mars seemed promising locations for great cities of strange inhabitants described by science fiction writers in fantastic ways. That they could have sinister designs on our planet added a bit of suspense. However, advances in astronomy and space exploration have shown that our planetary neighbors are not places that could give rise to or sustain such a thing. That "simple" life forms might exist on other planets or even moons is a slight possibility, but more than likely these life forms would be terrestrial in origin carried by solar winds and gravitational attraction to these distant places. There are a few *extremophiles* that could survive cosmic radiation and the vacuum of space.

Accounts of "alien abductions" are suspect and have only the most subjective of evidence and must be viewed with skepticism. Alien abduction narratives primarily rely on the testimony of individuals who have preconceived biases, are prone to misinterpretation, suffer from mental illness, or are outright fabrications. Sleep paralysis or nightmares explain at least a portion of these narratives.

As we have seen, the statistical possibility of alien intelligent life is as close to zero as it can get. Nonetheless, it seems many hope this earthly coil is not the sole habitation in the universe for intelligent life. Actually, it is often questionable whether or not there is intelligent life on this planet!

Moreover, that the possibility of UFOs or aliens being something sinister is a distinct possibility. There is some evidence that UFOs are diabolic in nature. They seem to do things that defy physics, such as flying at great speed and veering off at right angles without decelerating.

Dr. Hugh Ross, Christian astrophysicist, has at least one video on YouTube that explains the possible demonic nature of at least a portion of the UFO phenomenon. This can be found by searching "Reasons to Believe."

VI Sex and Gender: What Does The Bible Say?

Introduction

Sex and gender were ordained by the Creator from the very beginning. On Day Five (Gen. 1:20-23) God brought forth great whales, sea creatures of every type, and "winged fowl after his kind." He blessed them and said this: "Be fruitful, and multiply, and fill the waters of the seas, and let fowls multiply in the earth" (vs. 22). So, reproduction by means of sexual intercourse is ordained as soon as there are creatures which possess the proper "equipment."

On Day Six (Gen. 1:26-31), "So God created man in his own image, in the image of God created he him, male and female created he them. And God blessed them, and God said unto them, Be fruitful and multiply, and replenish the earth" (vss. 27 & 28). God concluded this, by declaring, "*It was* very good" (vs. 31).

So, sexual intercourse and the acknowledgment of two genders (male and female) are part of God's created order *from the very beginning*.

The second chapter of Genesis gives us another view of the Creation narrative. In a place called Eden, the first man, Adam, is given a task: "And the LORD God took the man, and put him into the garden of Eden to dress and keep it" (vs. 15). We see here the beginnings of economic activity. Since this is a garden with trees, it would seem the first job mankind pursued would have been that of agro-forestry. So, we would say that God appointed Adam to be a tender of His earthly garden.

However, Adam was not just a laborer, he was also given this important task: "to guard, protect, and hedge about the garden" (Heb. *shamar*). Even in this state of innocence, God had foreseen a looming danger to His perfect creation.

However, though Adam was obviously fit, his biological age was probably that of a man of about 25 or 30 years, and he had the fellowship of the Creator of the universe., nonetheless, he was incomplete. He needed a helper appropriate for his circumstances, and since he had also been commanded to "be fruitful and multiply," he needed an appropriate sexual partner, a female of his own kind.

God put Adam into a deep sleep and took a rib from his side. From this rib He fashioned a woman. Since she was taken from man (Heb. *ish*), she would be called *ishah*. Adam and the woman became a couple, and the God-ordained institution of marriage had its beginning (Gen. 2:21-24).

An institution is something of long-standing existence, and marriage is the *first* human institution. It predates the state. Hence, the state had nothing to do with creating marriage, therefore, it has no business redefining the institution of marriage, especially one designed and ordained by the Creator Himself.

That marriage is primarily concerned with reproduction ought to be self-evident. The modern world has cheapened marriage by making it an accessory, when marriage is part of the human obligation to the future. Traditionally, marriage was like an old-age pension plan. Children had an obligation to care for their aged parents, who had given their offspring the gift of life.

Of equal importance, is the passing on of traditions on to the next generation. For the Christian, that involves raising up children who respect God and His Word. After all, the Gospel is never more than one generation from extinction.

Hence, it ought to be self-evident that abortion is contrary to nature, reason, and to the Bible. Abortion is definitely an assault on the future. Moreover, it is the taking of innocent life, a violation of the Sixth Commandment, and of the six things the Lord despises, one is the "hands that shed innocent blood" (Pro. 6:17).

Gender and the Bible

It is evident that the Scriptures recognize only two sexes, male and female. Confusing of the sexes is contrary to Biblical norms. In Deuteronomy we read this: "The woman shall not wear that which pertaineth unto a man, neither shall a man put on a woman's garment" (22:5). It is evident that God is not the author of confusion (I Cor. 14:23), and to bring gender and sexual confusion into His created order is equivalent to idolatry (Lev. 18:22).

The operative word here is *confusion*. In the Hebrew the word is *tebel*, which comes from a word that means "to mix." However, in this sense *tebel* has the connotation of "an unnatural mixture." This is shown in Leviticus 20:12: "And if a man lie with his daughter in law, both of them shall surely be put to death: they have wrought confusion." This is part of a passage (vss. 10-23) that lists a number of acts that are capital crimes, such as incest and bestiality. But the underlying offenses are *against the natural order of things*

There is a natural role of the sexes taught in scripture. Men are called upon to be the leaders in the home and the church. He is to be a protector and teacher of what is right and wrong to his children. He to be honest in business and an honorable man in the community. Most importantly, the Christian man is to represent the Lord

Jesus to his family and to act as the family priest. To be the principal breadwinner for the family goes without saying.

There is equality between the sexes *in Christ*: "There is neither Jew nor Greek, there is neither slave nor free, there is no male and female, for you are all one in Christ" (Gal. 3:28). Now this verse does not mean Christianity has done away with the distinctions that make men who they are and visa versa for woman .

This is revealed in the following passage (Eph. 5:22-24):

> "Wives submit yourselves unto your own husbands, as unto the Lord. For the husband is the head of the wife, even as Christ is the head of the church: and he is the saviour of the body. Therefore as the church is subject unto Christ, so *let* the wives *be* to their own husbands in every thing."

However, submission is never a one way street, because we are to submit ourselves one to another "in the fear of God" (vs. 21).

131

Christianity is not like Islam. Women in Islam have a status below that of men. In many Muslim countries women cannot leave the home alone. Until recently, they could not legally operate a motor vehicle in Saudi Arabia. The testimony of a woman is only half that of a man in Islamic courts.

Women are not second-class citizens in the Kingdom of God. In spite of well-defined gender roles seen in scripture, Christianity operates under the principle of *grace*. Although we recognize that the Bible sets down some ironclad rules, for example, the Ten Commandments, nonetheless, we are not always bound to rigid standards. Jesus entire ministry was based on the superiority of grace over law: "For the law was given by Moses, but grace and truth came by Jesus Christ" (Jn. 1:17). This was affirmed by apostolic teaching (Acts 10:15; Rom. 4:27).

Biblical Sexuality

It is obvious that the Bible only sanctions heterosexuality. From the beginning God only recognized sexual relations between men and women within the covenant of marriage. Homosexuality is forbidden. This is affirmed in the Old Testament (Lev. 18:22; 20:13), and in the New (Rom. 1:27; I Cor. 6:9; I Tim. 1:10; Jude 7). Lesbianism, or sexual relations between women, is also contrary to nature (Rom. 1:26).

Now your *red letter* Christian will make this retort, "Jesus never said anything about homosexuality." Of course, our liberal Christian friend would be wrong. Christ affirmed the sexual morality of the Law. He said this, "Think not that I have come to destroy the law and the prophets: I have not come to destroy, but to fulfill" (Mt. 5:17). The Law forbids same-sex carnal knowledge, and the Lord here affirms the Law. He also declared, "For out of the heart proceed evil thoughts, murders, adulteries, fornications, thefts, false witness, blasphemies: (Mt. 9:19).

Adultery (Grk. *moicheia*) is unlawful sexual intercourse with the husband or wife of another. We call it "cheating," like it was subtracting strokes from one's golf game, or moving a chess piece when the other player is not looking. God has another mind on that. Adultery is a serious enough offense that it called for the deaths of both the adulterer and the adulteress under the Law (Lev. 20:10-12; Deut. 22:22-24).

Fornication (Grk. *porneia*) is illicit sexual intercourse, however, in this passage *porneia* is in the plural, that is, "sexual immoralities of all types." That would include homosexuality, lesbianism, pedophilia, and every kind of sexual activity not sanctioned by God's Word.

So, apparently Jesus *did* have something to say about homosexuality, and every other kind sexual immorality as well. Plus, because Jesus didn't specifically mention a particular sin does not mean He sanctions it. He didn't mention counterfeiting either, or a host of other crimes. Silence does not mean assent.

Marriage and then sex is the biblical norm. Marriage, according to Christ, is between one man and one woman for life. Divorce is forbidden, except in the cases of adultery (Mt. 5:31 & 32;19:19) or abandonment (I Cor. 7:15).

Multiple partners is also against the law of Christ: He says this, "For this cause shall a man leave father and mother, and shall cleave to his wife: and they twain shall be one flesh" (Mt. 19:5). Note, the Lord did not say that the many would cleave and become one. He said two-- one man and one woman--would become one flesh.

The polygamy practiced by kings, patriarchs, and men of means in the Old Testament is actually *polygyny*, or the simultaneous marriage of a man to multiple wives. Polygamy means "having multiple spouses." This could be either *polyandry*, or a woman having simultaneous multiple husbands, which is not the norm in polygamous societies, but is practiced in a few places, or the polygyny mentioned above. However, Christ knocked multiple marriages to the ground and declared the true intentions of the Creator from the beginning.   .

Conclusion

God created male and female and ordained sexual activity and heterosexual marriage from the very beginning. However, soon after the Fall human beings began to pervert the Creator's standards. Lamech, a descendant of the murderer Cain, "took unto him two wives" (Gen. 4:19). True to his murdering forefather, Lamech also shed blood (vs. 23).

However, while the full force of Adam's fall manifested itself fully in the line of Cain, the descendants of Adam through the line of Seth maintained godly standards for some time. However, that situation would not last forever. By the time of Noah, all of humanity had corrupted themselves except this man and his wife, three sons, and their wives.

The Deluge of Noah destroyed humanity and reset the world for a short time. It didn't take long for fallen humanity to begin perverting God's natural order of things once again. But the Incarnation of the Creator in the form of His only begotten Son reminds us of what He had planned from the beginning.

We have Christ and His Word to guide us on proper marriage, He doesn't lay out every principle to guide us in the matters of sex, gender, and marriage, but He has given us enough to light the path and keep us from straying from it.

Glossary Of Terms

Albedo: The fraction of light hitting an object that is reflected by that object, especially a planet, moon, asteroid, or comet reflecting the Sun's light   Albedo is measured from 0 (a black body that absorbs all sunlight) to 1 (a body reflecting 100 percent of sunlight). Earth averages an albedo of 0.3, the moon (0.12), Mercury (0.142), Venus (0.689), Mars (0.17), Jupiter (0.538), Saturn (0.499), Uranus (0.488), Neptune (0.492). Enceladus, a moon of Saturn, has the highest known albedo of any body in the Solar System at 0.99.

Abiogenesis: The hypothesis that life could come from nonlife. Disproven by the experiments conducted by Louis Pasteur in the 19th century.

Albigenses A heretical Christian sect that existed in southern France in the 12th and 13th centuries. In 1208 Pope Innocent III declared a crusade against the this sect. The Albigenses believed matter was evil. Many lived around the town of Albi from which comes the name of this group, also called the Cathars (from the Grk *katharos*, "clean" or "pure").

Aliyah: When Jews move to Israel from the *diaspora*. The word literally means "going up."   Leaving Israel by Jews is called *yerida*, "descent" or "going down."

Anabaptist: From the Greek, *ana*, "again," and *baptizo*, "baptize" ("to be baptized again"); a Protestant movement of the 16th century promoting the doctrine of adult baptism on the grounds that adults, or at least mature individuals, are the only ones who can make a proper decision to accept Christ as Lord and Savior and submit to baptism. They were opposed by Luther and others who held to the view that those who received infant baptism, even that administered by the Roman Catholic Church, need not be re-baptized. The Anabaptists would grow into the various Baptist denominations in existence today.

Anti-Semitism: A policy or attitude of discrimination or hatred for Jews. It reached its apex in Nazi Germany (1933-1945). This level of virulent anti-Semitism was continued by Arab nations after the UN partitioned the land on May 14, 1948. Only a fierce Jewish resistance and the intervention of God prevented a second Holocaust.

Cessationist: One who denies the permanency of spiritual gifts. Those who belong to this camp believe that spiritual gifts died out with the apostles or soon after and have not been, nor will they ever be legitimately revived. At least, that is their claim.

Chanukah: A Jewish festival marking the rededication to Judaism of the Temple in Jerusalem in 165 BC and celebrated by the kindling of eight lights. from 25th day of Kislev (the month of December), for eight days.

Charismata: Greek word for "spiritual gifts." Those graces which are a supernatural and sovereign bestowal for the purpose of edifying the church. There are nine such grace/gifts in the New Testament: (1) the word of wisdom; (2) the word of knowledge, (3) faith (4) healing (5) miracles; (6) prophecy; (7) discerning of spirits; (8) tongues; (9) the interpretation of tongues.

Diaspora: A dispersion of a people from their homeland, often used to refer to Jews collectively who don't reside in Israel.

Extremophile: An organism, especially microscopic, that is able to survive in extreme heat, cold, or in chemical toxicity that would kill other organisms.

Forces, Fundamental: Gravity, electromagnetism, weak nuclear force (radioactive decay), strong nuclear force (the strong bond holding the atomic nucleus together).

General Revelation: In theology, a limited knowledge of God perceived by observation of the natural world apart from the *special revelation* of Him by means of Holy Scripture.

Geocentric: Having the earth at the center of the universe. A cosmology first advocated by the astronomer Ptolemy in the 2nd century AD and shown to be incorrect by Galileo and others.

Glossalalia: The spiritual gift of speaking in tongues(from *glossa* "tongue," and *lalein* "to speak,") mentioned in Mk. 16:17; Acts 10:44-46;19:6, and described in Acts 2:1-13 and I Cor. 12-14. In Classical Greek, *glossa* is literally *tongue* (Latin, *lingua*). Secondarily, a language or dialect. However, in the NT the word in the plural is obviously used to indicate a supernatural gift given to a believer by means of the baptism in the Holy Spirit. According to the Scriptures, it is given to edify both the church corporately and the individual (I Cor. 14:1-4).

Hobby Horse: A toy wooden horse on rockers that gives the young rider the sense of motion without really going anywhere. The hobby horse is a fitting symbol for the response of some preachers who wax long, if not eloquently, on theological or doctrinal obsessions or pet peeves. The hobby horse of cessationists is their refusal to accept the plain reading of scripture--that spiritual gifts have been established for ministry

permanently in the church.

Mass: Physical quantity: the property of an object that is a measure of its inertia, the amount of matter it contains, and its influence in a gravitational field. Symbol: *m*.

Materialism: A theory of reality that all that exists is matter. God, spirit, and soul do not exist to the materialist. Reason, thought, and desires are explained entirely by physical functions. Many materialists even deny free will.

Natural Selection: Also called "survival of the fittest." The principle evolutionary process bringing about change of one species into another according to Charles Darwin. According to him, natural selection works because traits that favor survival in a species will be passed on by offspring, but unfavorable traits would lead to the elimination of those offspring.

Nihilist: An adherent of Nihilism, Russian political movement: a political movement in late 19th-century Russia that sought to bring about a socially just new society by destroying the existing one through acts of terrorism and assassination.

Non Sequitor: A statement that appears unrelated to a statement that it follows. A conclusion that does not follow from its premises From the Latin: "It does not follow."

Occam's Razor: The rule of philosophical or evidential simplicity: the logical and scientific rule that simple explanations should be preferred over more complicated ones, and that the explanation of a new phenomenon ought to be based on what is already

established fact.

Perspective: Appearance of distant objects to the observer, making them to appear smaller as the distance increases.

Pogrom: A campaign of persecution against a minority group, especially against Jews in Czarist Russia.

Red Letter Christianity: Christians who put the words of Jesus above those of the rest of Scripture. Actually, Red Letter Christians often set some of the words of the Lord Jesus above those of some of His other words, especially those that favor a *social gospel*. Hence, we could say the Red Letter Christian is more Red (Socialist) than Christian.

Secular Humanism: A philosophy or world view that stresses human values without reference to religion or spirituality. A type of *materialism*.

Social Gospel: A form of liberal Christianity that emphasizes feeding the poor, social justice, and wealth redistribution over that of preaching salvation through the death of Christ and His resurrection from the dead.

Transcendent: Existing outside the material universe, so not bound by it.

Ubermensch: The superior man or "superman" described by the German philosopher Nietzsche, and applied by Nazi ideology to the superior Aryan human being who is a member of the master race fitted by nature to rule over inferior human beings (the *untermenschen*).

Utilitarianism: The ethical doctrine that the greatest happiness of the greatest number should be the criterion of the virtue of action

Worldview: A world and life view, a paradigm or model of reality through which one sees and makes sense of the world.

Yellow Journalism: Sensationalist news reporting: a style of journalism that makes unscrupulous use of scandalous, lurid, or sensationalized stories to attract readers. (After the cartoon character *The Yellow Kid* that appeared in the tabloid *New York World*).

Zionist: A supporter of *Zionism*.

Zionism: a worldwide movement, originating in the 19th century that promoted the creation of a Jewish state in Palestine. Since 1948 the movement has shifted to supporting the nation of Israel.

References

Behe, Michael J.; *Darwin's Black Box: The Challenge to Evolution*; Free Press; New York; 1996.

Blumner, Robyn: "Give The Four Horsemen (and Ayaan) Their Due. They Changed America." *Free Inquiry* (4 December 2020).

Cohen, Ariel; Forbes.com; "A Bill Gates Venture Aims To Spray Dust Into The Atmosphere To Block The Sun. What Could Go Wrong?"; Jan. 11, 2021.

Davidheiser, Bolton; *Evolution and Christian Faith*; The Presbyterian and Reformed Publishing Company; 1969.

Dawkins, Richard; *The God Delusion*; Bantam Press, UK; 2007.

Eco, Umberto; *Foucault's Pendulum*; Picador; London, UK; 1990.

Faulkner, Dr. Danny R.; "Is Earth Flat?" Answers in Genesis, accessed July 2024.

_____ ; "Falling for a Flat Earth"; *Answers Magazine*; Nov. 1, 2018.

Freerepublic.com, "Imgur.com deleted this video clip of a jet starting and stopping a contrail. Why?";1/14/2025; Post 122.

Geisler, Norman; *Baker Encyclopedia of Christian Apologetics*; Baker Books; Grand Rapids, MI; 1999.

Guinn, Dr. Vincent P. ; *Testimony*; House Committee on Assassinations; Sep. 29, 2007; (Dr. Guinn testified that it was "extremely likely" the bullet was made by Western Cartridge Company fired from a Manlicher-Carcano rifle, the same type of weapon Oswald had purchased by mail order).

Hafner, Urs; "The Source of All Evil? *How a Bern Court Proceeded Against Anti-Semitic Conspiracy Fantasies in 1935*"; *Neue Zurcher Zeitung*; Dec. 23, 2005.

Huse, Scott M.; *The Collapse of Evolution*; Baker Books; Grand Rapids, MI; 1997.

Liddell and Scott; *Abridged Greek-English Lexicon*; Clarendon Press; Oxford, UK; 2001.

Louisiana vs. Clay L. Shaw; "Testimony of Perry Raymond Russo"; Feb. 10, 1969.

Kadzhaya, Valery; "The Fraud of a Century"; Dec. 17, 2005.

National Archives, Chap. 1; Washington D.C.; Sep. 24, 1964.

Norden, Eric; "Jim Garrison Interview"; *Playboy*; October 1967.

Penthouse; "Clay Shaw Interview"; November 1969.

Poli, Barbara De; "The Judeo-Masonic Conspiracy: The Path from the Cemetery of Prague to Arab Anti-Zionist Propaganda"; *Conspiracy Theories in the United States and the Middle-East*; De Gruyter; 2014.

Schlatter, Thomas; "Weather Queries: Chemical Controversy; *Weatherwise*; 9 March 2001.

Simons, Paul; "Weather Eye: contrail conspiracy"; *The Times*; (27 September, 2013).

Singerman, Robert; "The American Career of the Protocols of the Elders of Zion"; *American Jewish History*. 71 (1): 48-78.

Smith, Oliver: Chemtrails and other aviation conspiracy theories"; *The Telegraph. Archived*; (24 September, 2013).

Stroud, James; *Mere Christian Apologetics*; Tate Publishing; Tulsa, OK; 2017.

The Miami News; "Writer Not Sure Oswald Assassin"; Jan. 10, 1968.

Thomas, W. H. Griffith; *The Holy Spirit of God*; Wm. R. Eerdmans Co.; Grand Rapids, MI; 1964.

Vine, W. E.; *The Expanded Vine's Expository Dictionary of New Testament Words*: Bethany House Publishers; Minneapolis, MN; 1984.

Warfield, B. B.; *Miracles: Yesterday and Today*; Wm R. Eerdmans Co., Grand Rapids, MI; 1953.

Warshovsky, Fred; *Doomsday: The Science of Catastrophe*; Reader's Digest Press; USA; 1977.

Unger, Merrill F.; *Unger's Bible Handbook* An Essential Guide to Understanding the Bible; Moody Press; Chicago, IL; 1967.

Webb, Rob; "Did Man Really Land on the Moon?"; *Answers in Depth*; July 20, 2024.

www.ingramcontent.com/pod-product-compliance
Lightning Source LLC
Chambersburg PA
CBHW060800050426

42449CB00008B/1468